THE EVERYTHING KIDS' GEOGRAPHY BOOK

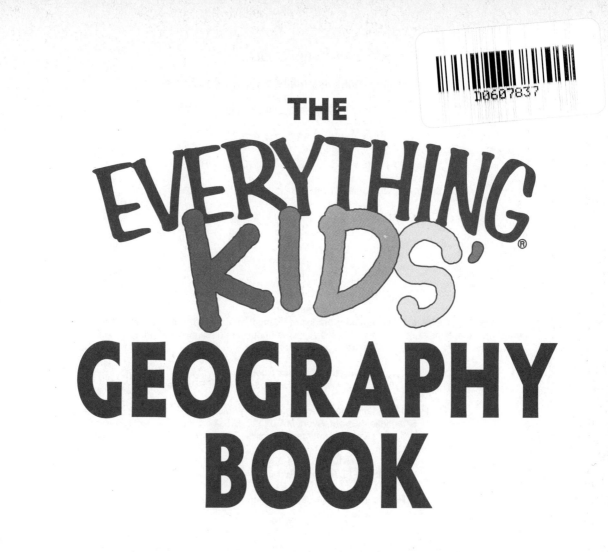

From the Grand Canyon to the Great Barrier Reef—
explore the world!

Jane P. Gardner and J. Elizabeth Mills

Adamsmedia

Avon, Massachusetts

PUBLISHER Karen Cooper

DIRECTOR OF ACQUISITIONS AND INNOVATION Paula Munier

MANAGING EDITOR, EVERYTHING SERIES Lisa Laing

COPY CHIEF Casey Ebert

ACQUISITIONS EDITOR Katie McDonough

ASSOCIATE DEVELOPMENT EDITOR Elizabeth Kassab

EDITORIAL ASSISTANT Hillary Thompson

An Everything® Series Book.
Everything® and everything.com® are registered trademarks of F+W Media, Inc.

Published by Adams Media, a division of F+W Media, Inc.
57 Littlefield Street, Avon, MA 02322. U.S.A.
www.adamsmedia.com

ISBN-10: 1-59869-683-1
ISBN-13: 978-1-59869-683-7

Printed in the United States of America.

J I H G F E D C B

This publication is designed to provide accurate and authoritative information with regard to the
subject matter covered. It is sold with the understanding that the publisher is not engaged in ren-
dering legal, accounting, or other professional advice. If legal advice or other expert assistance
is required, the services of a competent professional person should be sought.
—From a *Declaration of Principles* jointly adopted by a Committee of the
American Bar Association and a Committee of Publishers and Associations

Many of the designations used by manufacturers and sellers to distinguish their products are
claimed as trademarks. When those designations appear in this book and Adams Media was
aware of a trademark claim, the designations have been printed with initial capital letters.

Interior illustrations by Kurt Dolber.
Puzzles by Scot Ritchie.

*This book is available at quantity discounts for bulk purchases.
For information, please call 1-800-289-0963.*

Visit the entire Everything® series at *www.everything.com*

Contents

Introduction / vii

Dedication

To Jesse and Emmett—the question askers.
—J.P.G.

To my parents, who took me to Japan and opened up the world to me.
I am forever grateful.
—E.M.

Acknowledgments

I'd like to thank Gina Panettieri for her assistance and patience with this project. Thanks to the editors at Adams Media, especially Elizabeth Kassab, for the opportunity to work on this project. Many thanks to my coauthor Elizabeth Mills for her terrific work. Thanks to Diana for getting me started. Thanks to Jane Willan for providing the required moral support. And to Eric, for everything, as always.
—J.P.G.

Introduction

Long ago, people wondered about the size and shape of the Earth. They wanted to know what lands lay on other shores, who lived there, and what their lives were like. So they built ships to sail the seas and trekked across foreign lands to explore this big world. These explorers shaped the countries we know today, carving borders, establishing capitals, and settling cities.

But geography didn't end hundreds of years ago. There are geographers today who have the same curiosities. What does it take to be a geographer? It takes some special knowledge of Earth sciences such as biology and geology. It takes some knowledge of people sciences such as anthropology. Above all, it takes a deep desire to learn new things.

You hold in your hands a guide to the countries on planet Earth. You can read about England, China, Brazil, Kenya, Wales, the United States, and many other places. You'll learn about kangaroos and lions, penguins and camels, polar bears and pandas, geckos and blue whales. You'll meet all kinds of people from big cities and small villages. You can read this book from cover to cover or skip around from one chapter to the next. The important thing is to catch the travel bug and to always be curious about everything around you.

The next time you look at a globe, perhaps the world will feel smaller and more familiar to you. Spin the globe and let your finger stop it. Where did your finger land? Perhaps you will have a chance to travel to that country and meet the people who live there. What will you say to them? Think about how you'll describe your hometown and what you will learn about the country you're visiting.

Dear Parents,

Today's world is getting smaller and smaller. Television, the Internet, and other means of communication have linked us to people and events in other countries. This book is written to introduce your child to the big world out there. *The Everything® Kids' Geography Book* will take your child on a trip around the world. Each chapter will feature a different continent or region of the world, with an emphasis on the physical and cultural geography of the countries found there. Here are few of the things your child will read about in this book:

- the extreme temperatures of the Sahara
- the vast diversity of the Amazon Rainforest
- how the jagged peaks of the Himalayas and the Andes formed
- wildlife on Antarctica and near the North Pole

It is impossible to cover all of world geography in one book. This book is meant to spark your child's interest in the world and its people, animals, and landforms. Read the book with your child and discuss it. If your child is interested in a particular topic, guide him or her to other resources to find more information. Consider the following as you and your child explore the world of geography:

- use a map or an atlas to find the different countries mentioned
- introduce your family to the cuisine of a different country
- search the Internet for more information about the culture and the people of the world
- discuss the impact of climate and climate change on animals that live in different areas of the world

The possibilities are endless. We hope your child will develop an appreciation for the world around us as you read this book together!

—*Jane P. Gardner and J. Elizabeth Mills*

What Is Geography?

Whether you're already interested in geography or are just discovering it for the first time, you're going to love this book! Where else can you read about rainforests, volcanoes, penguins, and hurricanes all in one book? This book will take you on a trip around the world so you can look at the different continents and the countries that are found on them. You'll also take a peek at the people and animals living in these countries and what their lives might be like. Whether you are traveling north, south, east, or west, you will discover new and exciting things about the world of geography—but first you have to know what exactly geography is! There is probably more to it than you think.

Geography is the study of many different things. People who study geography think about the Earth, the things that are found on its surface, and the people, animals, and plants that live on it. Geography is the study of oceans, earthquakes, and mountains. It is the study of populations, food supplies, and climate. It is also the study of kangaroos, whales, and deserts. Geography takes all of these topics and looks at how they are related.

There are two main parts to the study of geography. The first is physical geography. Physical geography is the study of the surface of the Earth. This includes climate, mountains, oceans, and the plants that grow in these areas. The next part is cultural geography. Cultural geography is the study of the people on Earth. It is concerned with where people live and what their lives are like. The physical and the cultural sides of geography can be combined into one larger story about the entire Earth.

The people who study geography are called geographers. Geographers really need to know a lot about a lot of different things. They must know about different sciences such as geology and biology. That way they can understand what is happening on Earth and how it affects the creatures that live there. Geographers love their maps. They need to know how to read, interpret, and make maps. Geographers need to be good at math because they use numbers to track and record data. Geographers may also need to know about different cultures and people. And geographers today need to be able to use computers and other types of technology. Geographers help make decisions about worldwide issues. Maybe you will consider studying geography some day!

The Globe: Our Home

A globe is a small model of our home—Earth. It is a round ball with the continents and oceans labeled on it. It shows what the Earth looks like if you could travel out in space and look at it.

Most globes show the equator and the North and South poles. A closer look at a globe may show a series of lines. Lines that run vertically (up and down) on the globe are called longitude lines. Lines that run horizontally (left to right) are called latitude lines. Each location on Earth has its own unique set of latitude and longitude coordinates. This makes it possible to find any specific location on Earth.

The equator is an imaginary line that is found in the middle of the Earth. The equator has latitude of 0 degrees. It divides the Earth in half. The area above the equator is the Northern Hemisphere. The area beneath the equator is the Southern Hemisphere.

There are also Eastern and Western hemispheres. The Prime Meridian is an imaginarily line that travels around the world and passes through a city in England called Greenwich. The Prime Meridian has a longitude of 0 degrees. Locations east of the Prime Meridian

Fun Fact
GIS

GIS, or geographic information systems, is a technology that makes the study of geography easier. It uses computers, satellites, software, and other data to find patterns in geography. GIS is used to make and improve maps, globes, and models of places and things on Earth. It is one example of the way cool new technologies are helping the study of geography.

Where in the World?

Using a globe or a map of Earth, determine which two hemispheres you live in. If you are in the United States, you are in the Northern Hemisphere and the Western Hemisphere. What hemispheres is Australia in? What about Madagascar? Quiz your parents and see if they know!

Reading a Globe

Most globes have the continents labeled. Some even label the individual states of the United States. Find a globe in your home or classroom and locate where you live. What bodies of water are near your home? What other continents? Where have you and your family traveled to? Where have you read books about?

Reading a Map

Spend some time with a road map of your local area or your state. Use the map key to find the location of your school, local campgrounds or picnic areas, and lakes. You may discover things about your neighborhood or state that you did not know before.

(to the right) are part of the Eastern Hemisphere. Locations west of the Prime Meridian (to the left) are part of the Western Hemisphere.

Globes are usually placed on a stand and are slightly tilted to the side because Earth is tilted as well. Earth spins on an imaginary line called an axis. This axis is not straight up and down in space; it is slightly tilted. The Earth makes one complete spin on its axis in 24 hours. That is why our day is 24 hours long.

Some globes show more than just the continents and states. The oceans, large bodies of water, and mountains are often shown on globes. Some globes may even show the relief of the mountains, which means the mountain ranges may be raised or bumpy on the globe. This will make the globe seem more real. And there are globes of other places as well, not just of Earth. It is possible to find globes of the moon, the sun, even of the whole night sky.

Reading Maps

If you are going to study geography, you'll read a lot of maps. There are many different kinds of maps. There may be road maps in your family car. Mountain climbers use a special kind of map that tells them the elevation in an area. Engineers use maps to trace the path of a river or a location to build a new road. There are different maps for many different things.

Many maps have a key, or a legend. A key helps you read the map. For example, a map of your town may show your school, a set of railroad tracks, and the town park. The key at the bottom of the map will explain the colors on a map. Most of the time, water is colored blue on a map, and grassy areas such as fields or parks are colored green. Paved roads are usually black, while unpaved roads may be dotted or dashed lines. On a map key you will find symbols for hospitals, picnic areas, airports, and hiking trails.

There is even information to be learned from the size of the letters on a map. Usually, the largest letters go with the largest cities, those with more than 20,000 people. Towns that are written with smaller letters may mark a place with a population of 2,500 people.

Maps will also have a scale. A map scale helps you determine distances on the map. Think of a map as a scale model of an area. The map obviously cannot be as large as the actual location. It has to be scaled down to fit on a page of a book or a large sheet of paper. The scale may mean that one inch on a map is equal to one mile on the ground. That means if you were to walk a mile in your town, you would have traveled only an inch on the map. Seems like a lot of work for a little distance, doesn't it?

Sometimes many maps are put together into a book called an atlas. Many people have an atlas of the United

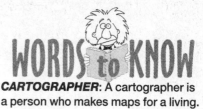

WORDS to KNOW

CARTOGRAPHER: A cartographer is a person who makes maps for a living. A cartographer practices the art of cartography, or mapmaking.

ELEVATION: The elevation of an area is its height above sea level. Sea level is zero feet. Anything above sea level will have a positive elevation. Mount Everest is the spot on Earth with the highest elevation. It reaches 29,029 feet above sea level.

Simple Symbol

Reading maps is simple once you understand the symbols. Can you match the real thing with the symbol? Careful, there's one extra.

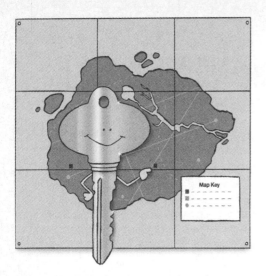

Finding the Distance

Find a map of your state or your hometown. Locate the map scale on the bottom. Then choose two places on your map that you want to determine the distance between. For example, you may want know how far it is from your house to the school. Or maybe you want to know how far it is from your hometown to your state's capital city. Use the map scale to determine the distance between those two points.

States in their car. It is a book of road maps of each state that can help them on their travels. There are atlases that show all the countries in the world as well.

How Many Countries Are There, Anyway?

There are seven continents on Earth. They are Africa, Antarctica, Asia, Australia, Europe, North America, and South America. This book will look at each of the continents in more detail.

It's hard to answer how many countries there are because not everyone agrees. The United Nations is an organization that is made of 192 countries. The U.S. State Department recognizes 194 countries. Others place the grand total at 195 countries. It all depends on what you count as a country. For example, the United Nations does not recognize the Vatican or Kosovo as countries. The United States recognizes both the Vatican and Kosovo as countries but does not recognize Taiwan.

A count of 195 countries may result if England, Scotland, and Wales are all listed as separate countries. Others lump those three together with Northern Ireland into one country, the United Kingdom. Sounds confusing, doesn't it? Don't worry. You are not alone in your confusion! Just keep in mind that people have agreed to disagree about the number of countries and go from there. There is still a lot of fun stuff to learn about the world!

Maybe it is not important to have an exact number of countries. It is more important to know that there are many different countries on Earth, each with its own geography. Organizations may argue over what makes up a country, but the bottom line is that the world is full of different people, places, and things. That is what the study of geography is all about.

The EVERYTHING KIDS' Geography Book

Mousey Messy Maze

It looks like one of the mice has lost his way.
Can you help him find his friend?

Mmmmmolten

If you want a nice cozy home in the earth, dig down. The closer you get to the center, the warmer it gets. But don't go too far; parts of the earth's core (which consists of iron) are so hot, they're molten.

How Geography Changes

Counting the countries seems easy compared to remembering the names of the countries. This is especially difficult because countries sometimes break up to form new, smaller nations, and other countries change their names.

If you were to look at a map from the 1970s, you would see counties called Burma in Southeast Asia, the Soviet Union in Europe and Asia, Zaire in Africa, and Czechoslovakia and Yugoslavia in Europe. A more modern map would show countries called Myanmar, Russia, the Democratic Republic of Congo, Slovakia, and Croatia. These are the new names for the "old" countries.

It is hard to keep track of the country names in all parts of the world. It is also sometimes difficult to know how to arrange the countries. There are seven continents, but some countries can be considered parts of two continents. Asia and Europe are part of the same land mass. The boundary between the two is not always clear, and sometimes countries are placed in both continents. The countries of Turkey and Russia can be classified as part of Europe and as part of Asia. Some countries do not seem to fit on any continent—New Zealand, for instance, is an island in the Pacific Ocean.

The important thing for you to remember is that the way countries are presented here is not the only way. There may be other ways to arrange the countries. This just shows you how geography is not exact. Geography is a changing subject. New information, advances in science, and politics can change your geography lesson.

Island I.D.

One way to tell land masses apart when you're looking at an atlas is their shape. Mark is happy he knows how to use shapes to tell these islands apart. He has to find the ones with five sides, mountains, and no lakes.
Can you help him?

Solo Tombolo
Sediment or sand connecting the mainland to an island is called a tombolo.

Across the Ocean

Before airplanes, there was only one way to get to faraway places.
Connect the dots to find out what it was!

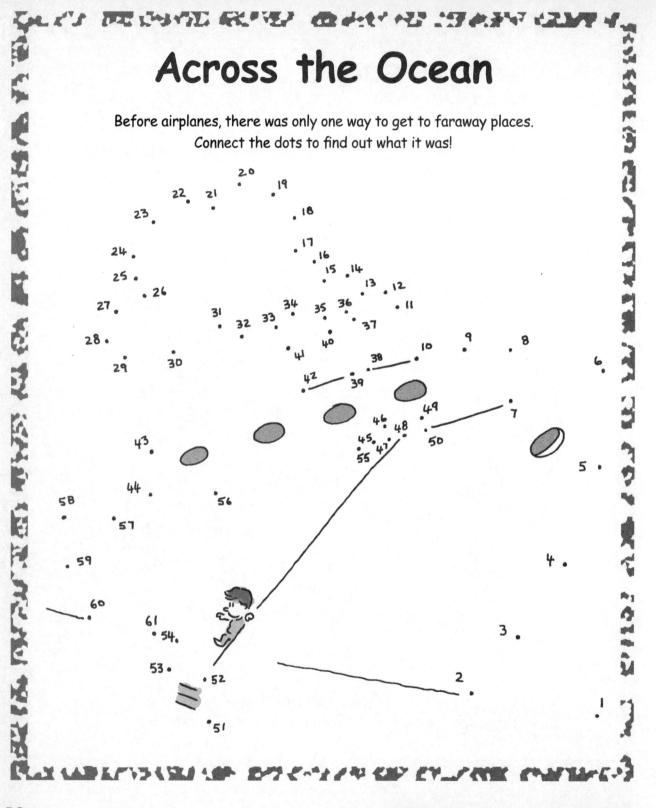

ALL ABOUT

the United States

Capital city	Washington, D.C.
Lowest point	Death Valley, –282 feet
Highest point	Mount Whitney, 14,494 feet
National holiday	Independence Day, July 4 (1776)
Population	304 million
Area	3.54 million sq. miles

New England

State	Capital	Nickname
Connecticut	Hartford	Constitution State
Maine	Augusta	Pine Tree State
Massachusetts	Boston	Bay State
New Hampshire	Concord	Granite State
Rhode Island	Providence	Ocean State
Vermont	Montpelier	Green Mountain State

Appalachian Trail

Land of the Free, Home of the Brave

Welcome to the United States of America, located between Canada and Mexico and between the Atlantic Ocean and the Pacific Ocean. The United States was originally settled by Native American peoples, and European settlers did not arrive until a few hundred years ago. That might sound like a long time, but it's nothing if you think like a geographer! People have come from all over the globe to work, study, and live here. The United States is the third-biggest country in the world in terms of land mass. Only Russia and Canada have more land. It also has the third-largest population in the world; only China and India have more people.

In this chapter you will learn about the states, the regions, and the landscapes that make up this great nation. You'll find out why the Appalachian Mountains aren't as high as the Rocky Mountains, what gave the Rockies their sharp peaks, and how the Great Plains got to be so flat. You'll also discover how different climates and terrains have shaped each region of the country. Let's hit the highway for a road trip around the U.S.A., from sea to shining sea!

Way out East

The first people to live in New England were the Algonquin-speaking Native Americans, including the Abenaki, the Penobscot, and the Wampanoag. The early European settlers in this area were English Protestants who wanted to be able to practice their religion freely without being punished by the Church of England. New England is famous for its authors, poets, and philosophers. The nation's first college, Harvard University, is in Cambridge, Massachusetts. It was founded in 1636.

Blizzards and Heat Waves

Seasons in New England are quite dramatic. In the fall, New England transforms as leaves everywhere

The **EVERYTHING KIDS** Geography Book

change color from summer green to autumn red, orange, yellow, and brown before falling and covering the roads and sidewalks. It's a very busy time of year for tourists who want to experience the beauty.

New England Industry

The land in New England is full of rocks, and the cold winters mean it is not the best for farming. Most New Englanders have had to find other ways to make money. They turned to the Atlantic for fresh seafood. Massachusetts's Cape Cod was named for the fish of the same name, and people in other parts of the country still drool over Maine's famous lobsters. Fishing is not as big an industry as it once was because there simply aren't as many fish as there used to be. Environmentalists say this is a result of overfishing—taking too many fish out of the water without giving them time to recover their numbers. Today, manufacturing and business are both major industries in the region, and the large numbers of colleges and universities employ many people.

Spotlight on Cape Cod

Cape Cod in Massachusetts is one of the most distinctive geographical features in New England. It's also one of the easiest to pick out on a map. It is a peninsula that looks like a long, skinny arm reaching out into the Atlantic Ocean. Cape Cod Bay is above the arm, the Nantucket Sound is below it, and Buzzards Bay is located in the armpit of the cape. Tourism is a major industry on Cape Cod, and visitors enjoy its many beaches.

The Mid-Atlantic States

Just south of New England are the Mid-Atlantic States. Settled by a wider variety of Europeans than New England or the South, the region continues to attract people of many backgrounds. From casinos and amusement parks to clambakes and Pennsylvania Dutch, the Mid-Atlantic region is a very interesting place.

Did You Know?

How Maple Syrup Is Made

During the cold months of February, March, and April, farmers in Vermont collect sap from their maple trees. They take the sap into a small cabin called a sugar house, where they boil it to remove the water. The sap becomes thick and dark. Now it's ready to be poured onto a big stack of pancakes! Vermont is the top producer of maple syrup in the United States.

WORDS to KNOW

PENINSULA: A peninsula is a body of land that is surrounded on three sides by water. The state of Florida is a peninsula. Can you find a state that is actually made up of two peninsulas? (Here's a hint: One of the peninsulas is shaped like a mitten.

ALL ABOUT
the Mid-Atlantic

State	Capital	Nickname
Delaware	Dover	First State
Maryland	Annapolis	Old Line State
New Jersey	Trenton	Garden State
New York	Albany	Empire State
Pennsylvania	Harrisburg	Keystone State

the Midwest

State	Capital	Nickname
Illinois	Springfield	Prairie State
Indiana	Indianapolis	Hoosier State
Iowa	Des Moines	Hawkeye State
Missouri	Jefferson City	Show Me State
Michigan	Lansing	Wolverine State
Minnesota	St. Paul	Gopher State
Ohio	Columbus	Buckeye State
Wisconsin	Madison	Badger State

Washington, D.C., is in the Mid-Atlantic area, but it is not a state so it doesn't have its own capital city or a nickname. But it is the capital of the United States, and it is home to the White House, the Washington Monument, the Smithsonian Institution, and other tourist attractions. More than 20 million people visit every year!

Peaks and Valleys

Long ago, glaciers came through the Northeast and created mountain peaks and river valleys. The Appalachian range is a chain of mountains extending from Newfoundland in Canada down to central Alabama in the southern United States, totaling 1,500 miles in distance. The range contains the highest peak in the Northeast—Mount Washington in New Hampshire. At 6,148 feet, the mountain is famous for its highly unpredictable weather and wind gusts of more than 230 miles per hour!

Travel down the rocky eastern coastline and eventually you'll hit the Hudson River Valley and the sandy beaches of New Jersey. The Jersey shore extends 130 miles along the Atlantic Ocean, and the beaches feature casinos, Victorian houses, boardwalks, and amusement parks.

Water, Water Everywhere!

Now let's go to the border between New York and Ontario. Be sure to put on your rain jacket! A collection of waterfalls sits between the twin cities of Niagara Falls, Ontario, and Niagara Falls, New York. Can you guess what these waterfalls are called? If you guessed Niagara Falls, you're right! The Canadian Falls drop 170 feet, and the American Falls drop 70 to 110 feet. More than 6 million cubic feet of water fall over the crest every minute during the day. The water is rushing very fast—more than 60 miles per hour at times.

Further south, near Baltimore, is the Chesapeake Bay, the largest estuary in the United States. Formed at the end of the last Ice Age, it's about 200 miles long and has 3,200 miles of shoreline. The Chesapeake is home to many fish, shellfish, and the famous Thomas Point Lighthouse.

The Midwest

Heading west through Pennsylvania, we enter Ohio and the Midwestern region of the United States. The Midwest and Plains states are sometimes referred to as the Heartland because they are located in the center, or the heart, of the country.

Industry

The Midwest has a booming economy. Big cities like Chicago and Minneapolis-St. Paul are major business centers, while farms in Wisconsin and Iowa grow crops that are then exported around the country. However, when the farming isn't as successful, places like Iowa change their industries to computer manufacturing or insurance. It's good to know how to do many things in order to be successful.

Mighty Rivers and Great Lakes

Waterways are very important to the economy in the Midwest. The Mississippi and Missouri rivers—the two longest rivers in the United States—are major routes for shipping and travel throughout the area. Minnesota's twin cities, Minneapolis and St. Paul, lie on either side of the Mississippi. The Mississippi and Missouri rivers actually meet each other near St. Louis, Missouri.

And there are transportation routes within the five Great Lakes (Michigan, Superior, Erie, Ontario, and Huron) as well. Locks, or water gateways, at Sault Ste. Marie, Michigan, enable ships to pass between Lake Superior and Lake Huron. These locks are among the busiest in the world. You could sail a boat around the Midwest even though you are not near an ocean. In fact,

WORDS to KNOW

ESTUARY: An estuary is a body of water where a river or stream meets the open sea. The Chesapeake Bay is where several rivers—including the Susquehanna, the Potomac, and the Rappahannock—flow into the Atlantic Ocean.

EXPORT: To export a product means to sell it to some other place. Illinois exports its cattle to other states in the United States.

LANDLOCKED: Places that are landlocked have almost no large bodies of water nearby. They are completely, or almost completely, surrounded by land.

WHAT IN THE WORLD

Michigan Wolverines?

The University of Michigan's mascot is a wolverine, and the state is nicknamed the Wolverine State. However, for about 200 years, no one had actually seen a wolverine in Michigan. In 2004, a biologist spotted a real wolverine near Detroit. Mystery solved!

WORDS to KNOW

INDIAN RESERVATION: An Indian reservation is an area of public land set aside for a Native American tribe to live on. There are more than 300 Native American reservations in the United States.

ALL ABOUT
the Plains

State	Capital	Nickname
Kansas	Topeka	Sunflower State
Nebraska	Lincoln	Cornhusker State
North Dakota	Bismarck	Flickertail State
South Dakota	Pierre	Mount Rushmore State

the best place to sail would be in Michigan—there are more boat owners there than in any other state! Minnesota is known as the Land of 10,000 Lakes, but it actually has more like 15,000 lakes. The word *Minnesota* comes from a Dakota word meaning "sky-tinted water." That's a good name, don't you think?

The Plains States

If we drive farther west, we come to the flat plains. Here, the winds blow hard with no mountains or hills in their path to block their force. These states are landlocked, so they have extreme seasons—hot, dry summers and bitterly cold winters.

Welcome to the Heartland

Imagine rolling prairies with rows and rows of corn, wheat, and soybeans growing in the hot sun. There are horse ranches and wide-open prairies all around. Open your eyes—you're in the Plains states! There were once many Native American nations—Apache, Dakota (Sioux), Cheyenne, and Comanche—hunting, living, and farming in these lands. Now they live on reservations scattered across the region.

Farmland and Badlands

Glaciers covered much of the Midwest during the last Ice Age, about 10,000 years ago. Their movement caused erosion and led to the flat, rolling landscape found in the Midwest. This resulted in excellent farmland with rich soil.

There are several rivers that cut through the Plains states—the Missouri, the Arkansas, and the Kansas. There are the North and South Dakota badlands, and in central Nebraska there are the Sand Hills—sand dunes held together by the grass growing on them.

Climb up into the Black Hills of South Dakota and you'll see four presidents' faces staring down at you. You've found Mount Rushmore! Each face is 60 feet high.

The sculptor, Gutzon Borglum, carved the faces into the hills from 1927 to 1941.

Down South

Point your wheels south and head on down to white sandy beaches in North and South Carolina, swamps and bayous in Louisiana, smoky mountains in West Virginia and Tennessee, wetlands in Florida, and prairies in Alabama and Mississippi.

Cotton and Conflict

The cotton gin was invented in 1793, and the production of cotton brought people to Alabama and Mississippi. This industry needed even more workers, so the plantation owners used slaves. The people in the Northern states were against slavery—they felt it was wrong to own a person and force them to work so hard without being paid or treated well. The people in the South, however, felt that slaves were necessary for their industries. This battle

WORDS to KNOW

BAYOU: A bayou is a small, slow-moving body of water that connects to a stream. Many fish live in bayous, such as crawfish (a kind of lobster), some shrimp, and catfish.

COTTON GIN: A cotton gin is a machine that can easily separate the fibers from the plant. It can work more quickly than humans can. The word "gin" is short for "engine," another word for machine.

Wacky Words

These Midwest farmers are taking a break after a long day in the fields. Can you figure out what wacky words they are singing? Figure out which letter finishes all the words in each sentence.

_ountain _oving _akes _en _iss _issouri.

_owardly _olorado _ows _hew _uds.

_ngels _re _ttracting _nts _t _rizona.

_hy _ould _ise _omen _ander _yoming?

_llinois _sn't _n _ndiana _s _t?

ALL ABOUT
the South

State	Capital	Nickname
Alabama	Montgomery	Heart of Dixie
Arkansas	Little Rock	Land of Opportunity
Florida	Tallahassee	Sunshine State
Georgia	Atlanta	Empire State of the South
Kentucky	Frankfort	Bluegrass State
Louisiana	Baton Rouge	Pelican State
Mississippi	Jackson	Magnolia State
North Carolina	Raleigh	Tar Heel State
South Carolina	Columbia	Palmetto State
Tennessee	Nashville	Volunteer State
Virginia	Richmond	Old Dominion
West Virginia	Charleston	Mountain State

the Southwest

State	Capital	Nickname
Arizona	Phoenix	Grand Canyon State
Nevada	Carson City	Silver State
New Mexico	Santa Fe	Land of Enchantment
Oklahoma	Oklahoma City	Sooner State
Texas	Austin	Lone Star State

led to the Civil War, which was fought between 1861 and 1865. When the South lost the war, the slaves were set free and the South was forced to rebuild.

Business in the South

Today, the South has lots of industries. The warm climate is ideal for growing oranges in Florida, rice in Louisiana and Arkansas, peaches in Georgia, and many other crops. West Virginia's main industry is mining, and North Carolina is the furniture capital of the United States. Along the Gulf Coast, fishermen catch shrimp and oysters to sell. The headquarters for Coca-Cola are in Atlanta, Georgia. Tourists flock to the South for food, history, and fun. Where would you go if you could visit a southern state?

All work and no play would make the South a very dull place, so let's see what fun things we can do. Horse- and car-racing are two very popular pastimes in Kentucky and North Carolina. The Kentucky Derby is held at a place called Churchill Downs. It is a one-and-a-quarter-mile race for three-year-old thoroughbred horses. In North Carolina, Lowe's Motor Speedway is home to the NASCAR Sprint Cup Series car races, where racecars zoom around an oval track. The South is also home to many different kinds of music, including blues and bluegrass.

Glades and Caves

Florida's climate is tropical, which means there is a wet season. And boy, is the wet season wet! It rains for seven months, from April to October, and much of the rain comes from hurricanes and thunderstorms. In southern Florida, there is a wildlife refuge known as the Everglades that depends on this wet weather. Many kinds of mammals, birds, reptiles, and plants live in the Everglades.

Heading over to Kentucky, we can walk, crawl, and wiggle through big and small spaces in Mammoth

The EVERYTHING KIDS' Geography Book

Mini Mountain

The state of Louisiana has some of the lowest land in America. In fact, its highest mountain is only 535 feet above sea level. It is called Driskill Mountain, but it doesn't actually qualify as a mountain because it isn't tall enough. How high do you think it would have to be to qualify as a mountain? There are a lot of mountains in this puzzle, but only two of them are real. Can you see which ones have one cloud, snow, two peaks, and the sun setting on the west side?

Hiding in Plain View

There are many towering mountains on earth that only a handful of people have ever seen, yet they are in plain view. How can that be?

Some mountains rise thousands of feet, but they never rise above the ocean they are sitting in.

Cotton Cash

Our dollar bills are 75 percent cotton. When the cotton fibers are processed, they become very strong. Hold a dollar bill up to the light. Can you see the fibers? Don't try and sew the bills together to make a shirt, though, it'll be too expensive!

WHAT
IN THE WORLD

bluegrass

Tennessee is called the Bluegrass State because its meadows and fields are covered with a grass that grows a blue flower in spring. Bluegrass is also a kind of music that features stringed instruments like guitar, banjo, and fiddle.

WORDS to KNOW

SLAVE: A slave is a person who belongs to someone else and must do what that person demands. Black slaves in the South belonged to white landowners who forced them to work on their land for no pay.

Caves, the largest cave system in the world. These tunnels and rooms were formed over millions of years by water and limestone. Always go caving with a friend or two to be safe!

Kentucky also has a magical secret—in Cumberland Falls State Resort Park, on a clear night with a full moon, you can see a colorful moonbow arc over the falls and the gorge. You can't find a moonbow anywhere else in the Western Hemisphere!

The Southwest

Now let's drive out to the dusty Southwest. Unlike Florida, very little rain falls here—less than five inches of rain per year—so the skies are sunny and clear all year long. Nevada is the driest state, with fewer than nine inches of rain or snow per year. The saguaro cactus loves this kind of hot, dry weather and can grow as tall as fifty feet. That's a big cactus!

History of the Southwest

The first people to inhabit the Southwest were the Pueblo—communities of Native Americans. They are famous for building adobe structures out of sand, clay, water, and sticks. The Navajo came next, and then Spanish settlers. In the 1800s, the area was controlled by Mexico. Although the region is now a part of the United States, the Hispanic influence is still seen today in the region's language, religion, architecture, and food.

In Oklahoma, in the 1930s, bad farming methods and a drought caused bad dust storms throughout the area. This gave Oklahoma the nickname "Dust Bowl."

The major industries of the Southwest include mining, technology, tourism, oil, and space travel. NASA opened its space center, called the Lyndon B. Johnson Space Center, in Houston in 1961. Astronauts train there and engineers monitor space missions from inside the Mission Control Center.

A Grand Landscape

The Colorado River has been rushing through the famous Grand Canyon for millions of years. The canyon is 227 miles long and about a mile deep. Temperatures and weather vary quite a bit here, making hiking tricky, but Grand Canyon National Park is one of the world's top tourist attractions with about 5 million visitors each year.

Over in New Mexico you can find the Carlsbad Caverns located in the Guadalupe Mountains. These caves were not formed by water and limestone like Mammoth Caves. Instead, they were formed from an acid called sulfuric acid. There are more than 100 caves in the Carlsbad Caverns National Park. Some of the caves have unusual names such as Balloon Ballroom, Chocolate High, Hall of the White Giant, and Spirit World.

Rocky Mountains High

Follow the Colorado River north up into the mountain states and the snowy Rocky Mountain range. Winter sports, such as skiing and snowboarding, are very popular here. Alta, a ski area near Salt Lake City, regularly gets more than 400 inches of snow each year! In 2002, the Winter Olympics were held in Utah and more than 2,000 athletes from around the world came to compete.

Climbing High

Catch your breath! The air is thin up here in the mountain states, especially as you go high into the Rockies. Many of the peaks stay snowy much of the year because the temperatures are always so cold. Mount Elbert, the tallest peak in the Rockies, stands at 14,433 feet. Colorado's average altitude is 6,800 feet above sea level, higher than any other

DID YOU KNOW?

Going Batty!

Austin, Texas, has the largest urban bat colony in the United States! About 1.5 million Mexican free-tailed bats gather at the Ann W. Richards Congress Avenue bridge. Batfest is a yearly event that features arts, crafts, food, music, and, of course, bats!

TRY THIS

Tex-Mex Eggs?

The next time you have eggs, try adding some chili powder. Chiles are a big part of a style of cuisine called Tex-Mex, which is popular in the American Southwest. It is a little spicy, so don't add too much!

State	Capital	Nickname
Colorado	Denver	Centennial State
Idaho	Boise	Gem State
Montana	Helena	Treasure State
Utah	Salt Lake City	Beehive State
Wyoming	Cheyenne	Equality State

state. The eastern side of the Rockies, however, is more arid, with grassy plains full of wheat and cornfields and cattle and sheep ranches. Southern Idaho also has rich farmland for potatoes, peas, and other crops. The economy out here features, as you can guess, farming, lumber, mining, cattle, and tourism.

Religion has played a big part in Utah. Mormons, as the members of the Church of Latter-Day Saints are called, settled in Utah in the mid-1800s. When Utah was admitted as a state into the United States, the church built a temple in Salt Lake City. The current temple is a popular tourist attraction. Mormons make up more than half of the population of Utah.

Wild Lands

Idaho has millions of acres of wilderness, more than any other state after Alaska. Much of the land is untouched and truly wild.

Montana is often called Big Sky Country because the land in the eastern part of the state is flat and open and it's easy to see the sky. The western part of Montana, though, is a different story. Glacier National Park features 2,000 lakes, dense forests, vast meadows, and more than 50 glaciers. While temperatures here can be mild in summer, they can dip well below freezing in winter.

Along the top of the Rockies in western Montana runs the Continental Divide. Rain that falls on the west side of the divide flows into the Pacific Ocean. Rain that falls on the east side flows out to the Atlantic Ocean.

Grizzlies, wolves, and a small herd of bison call Wyoming's Yellowstone National Park their home. The park is also famous for its geyser, Old Faithful, a hot spring that shoots steaming water up to 184 feet into the sky about every 80 minutes or so. Don't stand too close—the water is very hot!

Bryce Canyon and Zion Canyon national parks in Utah feature reddish, tan, orange, and white rocks that

are spectacular to see. Monument Valley also has red rocks as well as darker, blue-gray rocks. It sits inside the Navajo Nation Reservation.

This Is the West Coast

At last we've come to the West Coast. After all the deserts and wilderness, it's nice to look out over the big, blue Pacific Ocean. You can see surfers and sailboats and palm trees, but in the 1800s, people saw only gold.

Gold Rush

Gold was first discovered in California and Washington in the 1840s and 1850s and in Alaska in the 1890s. Once word got out, thousands of people hurried west as fast as they could, giving rise to the term "Gold Rush." Many arrived in covered wagons, as the Transcontinental Railroad was not yet finished. This great migration transformed California's population, which grew by an estimated 86,000 people in the first two years of the Gold Rush. Today, California is the most populated state, with a larger economy than any other state. Millions of tourists visit California every year.

West Coast Industry

Like the East Coast, the West Coast has its own seaport cities: San Diego, Los Angeles, San Francisco, Portland, and Seattle. And like the East Coast, these cities are central to the economic and commercial success of the area. Other regional industries include aviation, software, and agriculture.

Crash! Boom! Splash!

Ever wonder why earthquakes happen more on the West Coast than on the East Coast? California, Oregon, and Washington lie over two different parts of the Earth's crust. When those parts move against each other, they cause earthquakes.

ALL ABOUT
the West Coast

State	Capital	Nickname
California	Sacramento	Golden State
Oregon	Salem	Beaver State
Washington	Olympia	Evergreen State

Fun Fact

The first people who came out to find gold in California were called "forty-niners" for 1849, the year people outside of California came to seek their fortune. They also called themselves Argonauts, after the heroes of Greek mythology who searched for the Golden Fleece.

WORDS to KNOW

AVIATION: Aviation refers to the manufacture, development, and design of airplanes. In Seattle, Boeing is the major aviation company.

Fractured Faults

One of the main differences between the West and East coasts
of the United States is the fault lines on the West Coast.
There are fault lines out east, but the West Coast has many more.

Can you find the word **FAULT** in this puzzle? It is spelled correctly in five places. It can
go forward, backward, up, or down—but not diagonal. Careful, there are faulty versions!

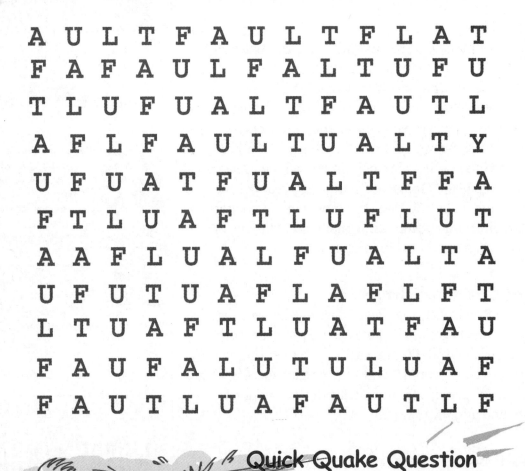

```
A  U  L  T  F  A  U  L  T  F  L  A  T
F  A  F  A  U  L  F  A  L  T  U  F  U
T  L  U  F  U  A  L  T  F  A  U  T  L
A  F  L  F  A  U  L  T  U  A  L  T  Y
U  F  U  A  T  F  U  A  L  T  F  F  A
F  T  L  U  A  F  T  L  U  F  L  U  T
A  A  F  L  U  A  L  F  U  A  L  T  A
U  F  U  T  U  A  F  L  A  F  L  F  T
L  T  U  A  F  T  L  U  A  T  F  A  U
F  A  U  F  A  L  U  T  U  L  U  A  F
F  A  U  T  L  U  A  F  A  U  T  L  F
```

Quick Quake Question

Q: Where was the largest earthquake
in the United States?

The largest earthquake in the United States was in
Alaska in 1964. It was measured at a magnitude of 9.2.

Volcanic eruptions have occurred here as well. The Cascade mountain range, which includes Mount St. Helens and Mount Rainier, are part of the Pacific Ring of Fire—a ring of volcanoes and mountains around the Pacific Ocean. The Cascade volcanoes are the cause of all recorded eruptions in the continental United States.

Alaska and Hawaii

Alaska and Hawaii were the last two states to be admitted into the union. They both became states in 1959 and are the only two states that are not connected to the rest of the United States. Those are some of the only things they have in common.

Alaska

Brrr! The snowy tundra in Alaska can get very cold in winter, especially on top of Mount McKinley, the highest peak in North America, which stands at 20,320 feet. Alaska has 17 of the 20 highest mountains in North America. During the summer, the sun is out all day and night and you can see the aurora borealis—colored lights that dance in the sky. Alaska is known for its beautiful landscapes and its wildlife, which includes moose, bison, elk, whales, eagles, seals, sea lions, otters, wolves, and bears.

Alaska is located right next to Canada, and it's closer to Russia than to the rest of the United States. Actually, Alaska used to be part of Russia. The Russians sold it to the United States in 1867 for two cents an acre. That might not sound like a lot, but Alaska is so big that it cost the United States $7.2 million! Alaska has more land than any other state and more coastline than all the other 49 states combined. But for such a big state, there aren't many people. Only three states have lower populations than Alaska. Alaska's economy depends on its oil pipeline and fishing trade.

Fun Fact

Sandcastle Day

Every June, on Cannon Beach in Oregon, people gather to make sandcastles. Some people are professionals, some are kids and families, and everyone has fun creating incredible sculptures out of sand.

ALL ABOUT

Alaska and Hawaii

State	Capital	Nickname
Alaska	Juneau	The Last Frontier
Hawaii	Honolulu	Aloha State

DID YOU KNOW?

Alaska

Before Europeans settled in Alaska, it was home to many different cultures, including the Eskimo and Aleut people. The name *Alaska* actually comes from a native word meaning "great land."

Hawaii

Hawaii's warm beaches feel nice after all that snow and ice. Hawaii is an island chain in the Pacific Ocean. All the Hawaiian Islands were formed by eruptions from undersea volcanoes. Mount Kilauea is Hawaii's most active volcano. It has been erupting since 1983, and you can see it if you go to Volcanoes National Park. What you won't be able to see is a new Hawaiian island called Loihi. It's still forming underneath the surface of the Pacific, and it will take tens of thousands of years for the new island to reach the surface.

Hawaii's islands have some interesting wildlife. Many of the birds on these tropical islands are brilliant reds and yellows. But there are also some familiar faces. Nenes look a lot like the Canada geese you might see on the mainland, and the two species are actually related. As you might guess, there's also a lot of sea life. Whales, dolphins, and sharks swim off the shore, and sea turtles lay their eggs on Hawaii's beaches. Hawaiian monk seals are an endangered species that are only found in Hawaii. Tourism is Hawaii's main industry, and pineapples and sugarcane are its main crops.

CHAPTER 3

Canada, Mexico, and Beyond:
Our Neighbors to the North and South

DEPARTURES
< gates 4,5,6

Provinces

Province	Capital
Alberta	Edmonton
British Columbia	Victoria
Manitoba	Winnipeg
New Brunswick	Fredericton
Newfoundland and Labrador	St John's
Nova Scotia	Halifax
Ontario	Toronto
Prince Edward Island	Charlottetown
Quebec	Quebec City
Saskatchewan	Regina

Territories

Territory	Capital
Nunavut	Iqualuit
Northwest Territories	Yellowknife
Yukon	Whitehorse

All about Canada

Capital city: Ottawa

Largest city: Toronto

Official languages: English and French

Area: 3.8 million square miles

Population: 33.1 million (2008 estimate)

Motto: "From Sea to Sea"

O Canada!

Canada is huge! It is the second-largest country in the world by size. It reaches from the Atlantic Ocean to the Pacific Ocean and up to the Arctic Circle. Its only neighbor is the United States, with which it shares its southern and northwestern boundaries. Canada is known for its large lakes, cold winters, and great hockey teams.

The Provinces of Canada

Canada is divided into regions just like the United States. Instead of being called states, these regions are known as provinces. There are ten provinces in Canada: British Columbia, Alberta, Saskatchewan, Manitoba, Quebec, Ontario, New Brunswick, Prince Edward Island, Nova Scotia, and Newfoundland and Labrador. There are also three territories in Canada: Northwest Territories, Yukon, and Nunavut.

What is the difference between a territory and a province? Provinces have their own governments and are part of the larger federal government of Canada. This means provinces make laws that are specific to them, laws on things such as education and the environment. Territories do not have that sort of individual power. They are also part of the federal government of Canada; they just don't have their *own* government to take care of more local issues. Provinces can also vote to change the constitution of Canada, while representatives from the territories cannot.

Rivers, Oceans, and in Between

Canada is a country of cities and wilderness. The population density in Canada is one of the lowest in the world. There are only about seven people per square mile on average. The population density of the United States is much higher, about 86 people per square mile. But this doesn't mean there aren't big cities in Canada! Cities like Toronto, Quebec City, and Ottawa are all places where

Discover Cove

Native people populated the area now known as Canada for thousands of years. The first people from Europe to "discover" North America are believed to have been the Vikings, as seen by settlements dating to approximately 1000 A.D.

They landed at L'Anse aux Meadows, Newfoundland,

a name based on the French for Jellyfish Cove.

There are seven coves on this island,

but only one of them is safe to land in.

It has two trees, one iceberg,

a river running into it, and a cave.

Water Water Everywhere

Canada has the world's longest coastline at 202,080 kilometres (125,567 miles).

WORDS to KNOW

POPULATION DENSITY: If you want to discuss how many people live in a particular area, you talk about the population density of the area. Cities will have a large number of people per square mile. Rural areas will have much lower numbers.

ALL ABOUT

Hudson Bay

Discovered by: Henry Hudson, 1610

Size: approximately 300,000 square miles

Average depth: 330 feet

Deepest spot: 900 feet

---

many, many people live and work. Canada also has a lot of open space. If you were to travel out to central or western Canada where the forests are thick, the mountains are high, and the plains are vast, you would definitely find more animals per square mile than people. The population density of bear, moose, caribou, and ducks would be way more than the population density of people.

The St. Lawrence River is a major feature of eastern Canada. It makes part of the boundary between the United States and Canada. This river flows northeast from Lake Ontario to the Atlantic Ocean. The St. Lawrence River is about 744 miles long, and many ships use this river route for trading and shipping.

The area where the St. Lawrence flows into the Atlantic Ocean is called the Gulf of St. Lawrence. This is the world's largest estuary. It is home to many different kinds of fish, and fishing has always been an important industry here. In the sixteenth century, European explorers hoped they could sail all the way to Asia on the St. Lawrence River. Sadly for them, the rapids on the river prevented them from getting any farther than present-day Montreal.

One of the largest geographical features in central Canada is Hudson Bay. Take a look at a map of Canada and you'll probably be able to find Hudson Bay right away. It looks a little bit like someone took a huge bite out of Canada! Hudson Bay is a huge inland sea in central Canada that is connected to both the Atlantic and Arctic oceans. Hudson Bay is home to many different kinds of animals including fish, seals, walruses, killer whales, caribou, and musk oxen.

The Rocky Mountains found in central and western Canada are part of the same mountain chain in the western United States. The highest peak in the Canadian Rockies is Mount Robson. It is in British Columbia and reaches a height of 12,972 feet. Mount Robson, like most of the mountains in the area, was shaped by glaciers that wore away rock and carved mountains during the Ice Age. Have you seen pictures of mountains with sharp edges or very pointy peaks? These peaks were carved by glaciers. There is still a glacier on Mount Robson named Robson Glacier.

Hola! Welcome to Mexico

Mexico is directly south of the United States. The official name of this southern neighbor is the United Mexican States, but most people just call it Mexico. Mexico reaches from the Pacific Ocean to the Gulf of Mexico. It has dry deserts just like the American Southwest, but it also has some of the most beautiful cloud forests and rainforests in the world.

Mexico City is the largest city in Mexico. More than 19 million people live in Mexico City.

Mexico is home to one of the longest rivers in North America. The Río Bravo del Norte is more than 1,000 miles long and forms the boundary between Mexico and part of Texas. You might be more familiar with this river by its English name, the Rio Grande. The river starts in Colorado and empties into the Gulf of Mexico.

Mexico has many mountains. The Sierra Madres are part of the same mountain chain that forms the Rockies in the United States and Canada. There is also a line of mountains formed from volcanoes that stretch from east to west across Mexico.

The Yucatan Peninsula is one region in Mexico. This region sticks out into the Gulf of Mexico. The land is fairly flat, and it is usually quite dry and hot. If you were to visit you might see jaguars, wild boars, monkeys, iguanas, parrots, and several types of large, dangerous snakes. The Sian Ka'an Biosphere Reserve is a protected area that takes up almost one-third of Mexico's Caribbean coast. It contains both ancient Mayan ruins and large numbers of wildlife, including more than 300 different bird species. Oil has been discovered in the Yucatan region, and it is an important export. Farmers grow crops such as sugarcane, corn, cotton, and coffee.

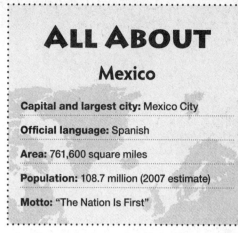

ALL ABOUT
Mexico

Capital and largest city: Mexico City

Official language: Spanish

Area: 761,600 square miles

Population: 108.7 million (2007 estimate)

Motto: "The Nation Is First"

Mexican Food

Did you know that most of what we refer to as Mexican food comes from the Yucatan Peninsula region? Barbeque pork, roasted chilies, and limes are some of the ingredients in Yucatan cooking. The next time you visit a Mexican restaurant, check out the menu. You may find that you are ordering food from this region of Mexico!

Mexican Marvel

One of Mexico's most interesting volcanoes is Paricutin, which erupted from the middle of a corn field in 1943. The local people couldn't believe their eyes. Here are some other things that are hard to believe.

Which center circle is bigger?

Stare at the blue dot and the haze will shrink.

Many of the foods you probably enjoy come from Mexico. For example, did you realize that tomatoes and avocados are native to Mexico? So are corn and vanilla. And the thing that many people (maybe you) love more than any other—chocolate—comes from Mexico, too.

Mexico is home to many animals, plants, and different types of crops. Mexico supports at least 10 percent of the world's biodiversity! There are many different mammals, birds, insects, reptiles, and plants in this country.

Come Visit the Caribbean, Mon!

The islands of the Caribbean are part of North America as well. There are more than 7,000 islands in this region of the world! The islands are part of an archipelago that forms a boundary around the Caribbean Sea. The Caribbean Islands are known for their tropical waters and beaches, but there is much more to know. So pack your bags for a visit to three of the Caribbean Islands!

Cuba: The Largest Caribbean Island

Cuba is the largest island in the Caribbean; it is the seventeenth-largest island in the world. What we think of as Cuba is actually several islands together. Cuba is located between the Caribbean Sea, the Gulf of Mexico, and the Atlantic Ocean. The island is about 90 miles from the tip of Florida.

Cuba has it all! There are flat rolling plains on the island as well as high peaks. The mountains in the southern part of the island are steep. The highest peak in this chain of mountains

The EVERYTHING KIDS Geography Book

is Pico Real del Turquino, about 6,476 feet high. This mountain, as well as others in the area, has many mineral deposits—copper and iron, among others, are mined here.

Cuba has what many people would call the perfect climate—if you like warm days with a tropical breeze all year long. The average temperature in January is 70 degrees. In July the average temperature is 80 degrees.

Cuba has a rainy season lasting from May to October and a dry season from November to April. This is related to hurricane season. Cuba is in the path of many of the hurricanes that form in the Atlantic Ocean. It is often hit by these fierce storms, which bring heavy rains and strong winds to the island.

Jamaica: Ready for Some Reggae?

Jamaica is the third-largest island in the Caribbean, but it has the most people of any island in the area. Every year, many people from the United States and the rest of the world head to Jamaica for vacation.

Most of the island is covered in mountains, but the small flat area around the coast boasts some beautiful beaches. Jamaica's Blue Mountains have very good soil for growing crops. Coffee from the Blue Mountains is quite famous and can be found for sale in many places—maybe even in your local grocery store!

Jamaica is famous for its botanical gardens. Much of the island has been set aside for national parks or preserved areas. The Royal Botanical Gardens were originally donated by one family in celebration of the abolition of slavery; they're "royal" because Great Britain's Queen Elizabeth II enjoyed her visit in 1953 so much that they were renamed in her honor.

Jamaica is often hit by hurricanes. One of the worst hurricanes to hit Jamaica was Hurricane Gilbert in September 1988. More than 27 inches of rain fell on Jamaica during the storm and nearly fifty people were killed when it hit Jamaica. Countless homes, crops, and businesses were destroyed.

ALL ABOUT
Cuba

Capital and largest city: Havana

Area: 44,200 square miles

Population: 11.2 million

Motto: "Fatherland or Death"

All about Jamaica

Capital and largest city: Kingston

Area: 4,244 square miles

Population: 2.67 million (2006 estimate)

Motto: "Out of Many, One People"

WORDS to KNOW

BOTANICAL GARDEN: A botanical garden is a special type of garden. Many different types of plants and flowers are grown here. Botanical gardens are often used to teach people. These places are usually open for visitors so that people may come and enjoy nature.

Nutmeg

There is a nutmeg on Grenada's flag. This is because it is the island's most important export. In fact, Grenada supplies approximately 20 percent of the world's supply of nutmeg. Think of this tiny island nation the next time you have a piece of pumpkin pie or a gingerbread cookie!

Grenada

The country of Grenada, located in the southern part of the Caribbean, is made up of three main islands. The largest island is called Grenada, and this is where most of the population lives. This part of the Caribbean is not hit by hurricanes as often as some of the other islands. Hurricanes do move over the island, but it is not a yearly event as it is in some places.

Grenada was formed by volcanoes. This makes the soil very fertile and good for growing crops. Grenada is known for its sugar crops. It is sometimes called "Spice Island." Many spices, such as cinnamon, cloves, ginger, and nutmeg, are grown on the island. These are the main exports for the country.

Grenada is divided by a mountain range. Mount St. Catherine is the highest peak, reaching more than a mile and a half into the air. Many rivers and waterfalls cover the area, and there are also deep gorges and some of the best beaches in the world.

Shape Shifter

This is an archipelago of islands, just like in the Caribbean. But something terrible has happened: All the water has been drained out of each lake. Can you put them back in their proper places?

Is Greenland Really Green?

Look on a map of North America. Notice that large island way up in the northeastern part of the continent? This is the island of Greenland, the largest island in the world.

Greenland's Climate

Greenland is very cold. A typical day on Greenland may see temperatures around 14 degrees. It feels really warm on Greenland when it reaches into the fifties. Greenland is also very dry, so there is little snow.

Almost the entire island is covered in a giant sheet of ice. In some places, the ice can be nearly two miles thick! These giant ice sheets, or glaciers, sometimes slide along the continent until they reach the ocean. When the ice hits the ocean, icebergs form. The giant ice sheets and icebergs in Greenland make up nearly 10 percent of all the fresh water on Earth. That's a lot of frozen ice cubes!

If most of the island is covered in ice, how did Greenland get its name? If you hopped in your Viking ship and sailed for Greenland, the first part of the island you would see is the coast. The coastline is rocky, mountainous—and very green! This is why the island is called

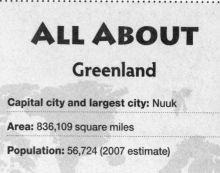

ALL ABOUT
Greenland

Capital city and largest city: Nuuk

Area: 836,109 square miles

Population: 56,724 (2007 estimate)

CALVING: Calving is when icebergs break off a larger ice sheet. Only a small part of the whole iceberg sticks up out of the water as it floats away. That is where the phrase "just the tip of the iceberg" comes from. It means that there is a lot more that can't be seen!

Noisy Ice

Glaciers and icebergs can be very noisy. Drop several ice cubes into a glass of warm water. You may notice how they crack and make a popping noise when they do so. This is the same sound icebergs make as they fall off into the ocean—only icebergs are much, much louder!

ALL ABOUT

Central America

Country	Capital
Belize	Belmonpan
Costa Rica	San José
El Salvador	San Salvador
Guatemala	Guatemala City
Honduras	Tegucigalpa
Nicaragua	Managua
Panama	Panama City

All about Nicaragua

Capital and largest city: Managua

Area: 59,998 square miles

Population: 5.4 million (2005 estimate)

Greenland, even though the rest of the island does not exactly live up to its name. If you measured the length of the coastline of Greenland, you would find it is almost as long as the length of the equator!

During some months there are parts of Greenland that stay dark all day long, but during the summer, the opposite happens. There are days with no nights! Why do you think this is? You've probably noticed that it gets darker earlier during the winter than in the summer. The same thing happens in Greenland—it's just more extreme. In the winter, the Northern Hemisphere of the Earth is farther away from the sun, so it gets darker earlier. The farther north you are, the less light from the sun gets to you. In the summer, the Earth's orbit changes, and the Northern Hemisphere is angled toward the sun.

Where Is Central America?

Central America is just where its name says should be. It is an isthmus between North and South America. There are seven countries that make up Central America.

Central America is geologically active. This means that there have been many earthquakes and volcanoes here. Central America is a region of the world known for its biodiversity as well. Let's take a look at the largest of these beautiful countries.

Nicaragua

The name Nicaragua comes from the name of a local tribe and the word *agua*, which means water. There is much water in this country, including large lakes, rivers, lagoons, and ponds.

Nicaragua can be split into three different regions. The area that borders the Atlantic Ocean is a rainforest. This area is known as the Atlantic lowlands. The largest river in Central America, the Río Coco, is located here. The area that borders the Pacific Ocean is known as the Pacific lowlands region.

The middle part of Nicaragua is mountainous. This area is called the central highlands. Many different types of animals and plants can be found in this area, and there are hazy cloud forests where water comes in the form of thick fog instead of rain or snow. The area is known for its abundance of birds, including the resplendent quetzal, goldfinches, and colorful toucans. The soil here is very good for growing crops, including coffee.

There are many national parks and preserves in Nicaragua. The Bosawas Biosphere Reserve is one of them. This preserve is located in the northern part of Nicaragua. It is one of the largest rainforests in North and South America. Only the Amazon is larger. This preserve takes up nearly 10 percent of the total land area in Nicaragua.

The biodiversity in the Bosawas Biosphere Reserve is mind boggling. Some people guess there are between 10,000 and 20,000 species of insects there—and that's just the bugs. Many other animals call the reserve home, too. Visitors have seen puma, jaguars, quetzals, and harpy eagles. In fact, much of this area has not been explored yet, so there could be more species that no one has ever seen!

WORDS to KNOW

ISTHMUS: An isthmus is a narrow bit of land that connects two large land bodies. Look at a map. You will see how North America and South America are connected by a thin strip of land. This thin strip is Central America.

CLOUD FORESTS: A cloud forest could also be called a "fog forest." These are forests that are found on high mountain peaks, where the clouds seem to hang over the region. Ferns, rich soils, and drizzly conditions dominate these forests.

WHAT IN THE WORLD

What is a resplendent quetzal?

A resplendent quetzal is a bird found in Nicaragua and other Central American countries. Its tail can be nearly twice as long as the rest of its body! These noisy, fruit-eating birds usually have a green body and a red breast.

The Fastest Game on Earth

It looks like this player is all suited up and ready to play his favorite game—which also happens to be one of the most popular sports in Canada. Connect the dots to find out what it is!

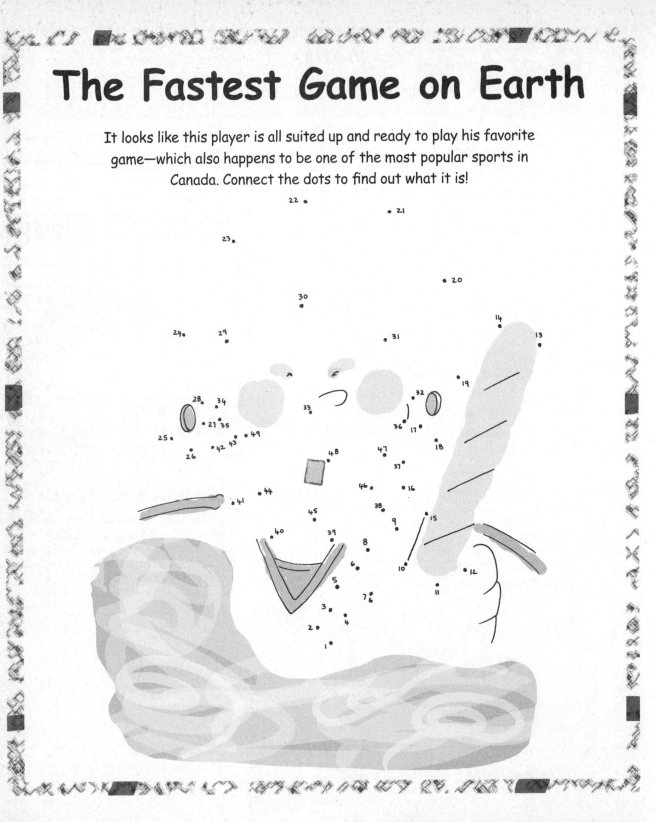

ALL ABOUT
South America

Country	Capital
Argentina	Buenos Aires
Bolivia	La Paz
Brazil	Brasília
Chile	Santiago
Colombia	Bogotá
Ecuador	Quito
Guyana	Georgetown
Paraguay	Asunción
Peru	Lima
Suriname	Paramaribo
Uruguay	Montevideo
Venezuela	Caracas

WORDS to KNOW

WILLIWAW: Williwaw is the name for the winds that sometimes come up from nowhere around the tip of South America and in other regions. Williwaw winds are sudden and are created by wind howling down from mountains to the ocean. The cold air from the snow-covered mountains rushes down and often knocks boats on their side.

The Land below the Equator

South America stretches all the way from the equator to the South Pole. It is home to the largest rainforest on the planet and some of the highest, most treacherous mountains as well. Volcanoes dot the western boundary of South America, and rolling beaches are found on the eastern coast.

South America is surrounded by water. The Atlantic Ocean forms the eastern boundary and the Pacific Ocean forms the western boundary. Part of the northern boundary is formed with Central America while the rest is bounded by the Caribbean Sea. South America is part of the region that historians refer to as the New World. It was first mapped by Europeans in 1507 as explorers came to realize that this area was not part of North or Central America.

Cape Horn Island is the southernmost spot of South America. It is known for severe winds, harsh weather, and hazardous conditions. In the past, sailors and traders trying to reach the Pacific Ocean from the Atlantic had to travel the dangerous path around Cape Horn. They would often encounter williwaw winds. This was the only path around South America until the Panama Canal opened in 1914. The Panama Canal provided shippers, sailors, and traders a passage between the Atlantic and the Pacific.

Land of Extremes

There is a lot of variety within South America. We'll explore Brazil, the largest country in South America, and Suriname, the smallest.

Brazil

Brazil is the largest country in South America by size. It makes up just about half of the entire continent of South America! Brazil is located in the Northern Hemisphere, the Southern Hemisphere, and the Western Hemisphere. The equator crosses Brazil, so some of the country is in the Northern Hemisphere, and some of it is in the Southern Hemisphere.

If you compare South America and Africa, you might notice that it looks like the eastern part of Brazil fits into the western part of Africa. This isn't just a coincidence. Long ago, when all of the continents were joined in one massive continent, called Pangaea, South America and Africa fit together like two giant puzzle pieces. Over time, the tectonic plates shifted and the two continents separated from each other because they were on different plates.

Brazil has one of the highest populations in the world. In fact, by 2008 estimates, Brazil has the fifth-highest population in the world! This is may seem strange when you consider that much of the country is covered in rainforests. It just means that the population density in the cities along the coastal regions of Brazil is quite high. Most of Brazil's cities are located on the Atlantic coast or near the big rivers. The Atlantic coast is generally made up of lowlands that quickly rise up to a higher plateau. In southern Brazil, the plateau turns into wide plains. Farther north, the Serra do Mar mountains erupt from the plateau.

Iguaçu Falls mark the spot where Brazil, Argentina, and Paraguay meet. Iguaçu means "big water," and these waterfalls certainly live up to their name! About 150 waterfalls make up Iguaçu Falls—and that's during the dry season. With heavy rains, that number can double to 300! Most of the waterfalls are on the Argentinean side, which means you get the best views of the falls if you stand on the Brazilian side. Fourteen waterfalls make up the horseshoe-shaped Devil's Throat, one of the most impressive parts of the falls. It plunges 350 feet—more than twice as far as the biggest waterfall at Niagara Falls in North America.

Brazil has rainforests, beaches, and beautiful rivers. The Amazon Rainforest, the largest rainforest in the world, is located partially in Brazil. Beaches line the

Fun Fact

How Big Is Brazil?

Brazil is so large that it shares a border with every South American country except two—Ecuador and Chile.

WORDS to KNOW

TECTONIC PLATES: The Earth's crust is divided into seven major tectonic plates and many other small ones. The surface of the Earth changes slowly over many millennia as the plates move. The areas where the plates meet are often the locations of earthquakes, volcanoes, and mountains.

Make the Rain Fall

Rainforests are amazing places. They are like giant sponges that soak up the rain. Some of the water evaporates, which causes clouds to form, and then more rain falls.

Here's a fun experiment you can try to see the cycle in action. You'll need a cup, a baggie, some tape, and some water.

1. Fill the cup with water and put it inside the baggie.
2. Close the baggie and tape it shut.
3. Place the baggie in a sunny window.

Can you see what happens? The sun's heat will evaporate the water from the cup (the water particles are so small you can't see them). Then it condenses inside the bag— back into water. These water droplets fall down, just like rain.

Do Good

You can buy an acre of rainforest and save it from being cut down. Just visit www.worldlandtrust.org.

I own 1 acre of Rainforest.

The EVERYTHING KIDS' Geography Book

Atlantic coast of Brazil in cities such as Rio de Janeiro. Brazil has hot, humid weather in many places. Since most of the country is located near or around the equator, the country is typically quite tropical.

One of most significant threats to the country is deforestation, the loss of natural forests. People cut down the trees so they can use the rich soil to grow crops and make money, but this comes at a cost to the environment. This practice threatens the plant and animal life living in the Brazilian rainforest. Other dangers to the area include air and water pollution near the larger cities in Brazil. There is also a large illegal wildlife trade in the rainforests. This practice of removing wildlife from its natural habitat and selling it to others is very lucrative for the poachers but very harmful for the survival of the animals.

Suriname

Suriname, located in northern South America, is the continent's smallest country. If you look at an older map or atlas, you may see Suriname listed as Nederlands Guyana. That's because it used to be a colony of the Netherlands, and it gained its independence in 1975. Today, the country's official name is the Republic of Suriname, although most people refer to it by its shorter name.

Suriname exports quite a few goods and crops to other parts of the world. Bananas and rice are two of the most significant agricultural exports. Suriname also has valuable mineral resources, including bauxite, gold, and some petroleum products. Suriname has an abundance of fish and shrimp, and this small country is a leader in the production of hydropower.

Suriname borders Brazil to the south, and its geography is similar to Brazil's. Most of its population lives on the Atlantic coast, and the country's interior is mostly covered in tropical rainforests. Timber from these forests is one of Suriname's top exports, and deforestation is one of the country's most serious environmental challenges, just as it is in Brazil.

Animals in Brazil

Did you know that Brazil is a world leader when it comes to biodiversity? Brazil is home to the largest number of different primates and mammals and the third-highest number of birds in the world.

ALL ABOUT

All about Suriname

Capital and largest city: Paramaribo

Official language: Dutch

Area: 63,037 square miles

Population: 492,829 (2004 census)

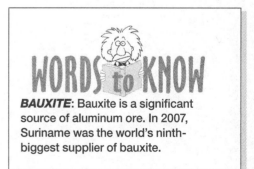

BAUXITE: Bauxite is a significant source of aluminum ore. In 2007, Suriname was the world's ninth-biggest supplier of bauxite.

Suriname has a very hot, tropical climate. The average temperature in this small country does not vary much throughout the course of the year. There are basically two seasons here—the wet season and the dry season. The wet seasons last from April to August and from November to February. Dry seasons fall in between, from August to November and February to April. A visit to Suriname would provide an opportunity to explore many different areas. For example, the Galibi Nature Reserve is a beach nature reserve. There you could see giant leatherback sea turtles lay their eggs from April to August. The reserve is also a place where the green hawksbill hatch their eggs. In the Raleighvallen Nature Reserve you could take a challenging hike through the jungle to reach a magnificent waterfall on the Coppename River. Maybe you'd spot some of the many different species of birds and monkeys that live there. Mount Kasikasima, in the southern part of Suriname, rises higher than 2,300 feet. Traveling to Mount Kasikasima involves a trip in a canoe for several days and then a climb to the top. It is a beautiful granite mountain with spectacular views of the country and its wildlife.

Mountains, Waterfalls, and Rainforests

South America holds the world's records for many geography-related topics. Take a look at the South America's records:

- world's largest river by volume: Amazon River
- world's highest waterfall: Angel Falls
- world's longest mountain range: the Andes

Fun Fact

French Guiana

If you look at a map of South America, you might see a place labeled French Guiana right next to Suriname, and you might think, "Hey, that looks smaller than Suriname!" You're right. French Guiana is a little more than half the size of Suriname—but it is part of France. Suriname is the smallest independent country in South America.

The EVERYTHING KIDS' Geography Book

- world's driest desert: Atacama Desert
- world's biggest rainforest: Amazon Rainforest
- world's southernmost town: Puerto Toro, Chile
- world's capital at highest elevation: La Paz, Bolivia

Angel Falls

Venezuela's Angel Falls is the world's largest free-falling waterfall. The water drops from a height of 3,212 feet!

Angel Falls was named for an American named Jimmie Angel. People native to the area had known about the falls for a long time, but Angel, an American pilot, flew his plane over this area in search of gold deposits in the 1930s. His plane got stuck and he and his companions had to hike out of the area. On this trek, they stumbled upon Angel Falls.

Tierra del Fuego

The southern part of South America is made up of fjords like the ones in northern Europe. At the very southern tip of the continent is an archipelago called Tierra del Fuego. Its name means "land of fire," and it got this name from Ferdinand Magellan's crew, who saw the fires the native people built to keep themselves warm.

Part of the Tierra del Fuego archipelago belongs to Chile; the other part belongs to Argentina. This area has a very harsh climate. There are glaciers that reach all the way from the mountaintops to the ocean. Snow falls year round in some parts of the archipelago. Long winters, short summers, lots of rain, and very windy conditions make life difficult. Many of the people who live in this area make their living from sheep farming.

Tierra del Fuego is known for its amazing wildlife. In the sea, you can see walruses and seals and many different types of sea birds. On land, you will find North American beaver, European rabbits, and reindeer from the Arctic! People introduced these animals to this area,

Fun Fact

Water in the Air

The water from the top of Angel Falls never actually reaches the ground. The water has to fall such a great distance that strong winds turn it into mist.

WORDS to KNOW

ARCHIPELAGO: An archipelago is a chain of islands. Archipelagos are usually found in open water, such as an ocean or sea. There are archipelagos in the Pacific Ocean, in the Caribbean, and in the northern Atlantic Ocean.

American Records

South America is home to a number of world-record geographic features: Angel Falls, the world's highest waterfall; the Amazon River, the world's largest river (by volume); and the Amazon Rainforest, the world's largest rainforest. That's a lot of records! There's another world record that has to do with a place called Atacama. Can you see what it is? Just remove all of the letters but E, I, R, T, D, and S.

M	B	J	D	A	F	Y	P	C	U
R	C	A	O	N	P	I	H	P	G
O	E	w	B	O	A	S	T	b	Z
C	H	Q	D	U	F	N	L	a	E
S	G	Y	f	G	Y	H	E	Q	F
P	F	g	R	A	p	V	T	U	A

Joking Geography

A tourist is admiring an ancient volcano when his guide tells him it is exactly 2,003 years old. The impressed tourist asks how he knows so precisely. "Well," the guide replies, "the geography professor said it was 2,000 years old, and that was 3 years ago."

The EVERYTHING KIDS' Geography Book

but the results have not been good. These animals, which are not native to the area, have destroyed many of the local plants and have changed the natural ecosystems.

The Andes

The Andes are found along the west coast of South America. They are more than 4,400 miles long, stretch as wide as 300 miles in places, and reach an average height of 13,000 feet above sea level. The Andes pass through seven of the twelve South American countries: Argentina, Chile, Peru, Bolivia, Venezuela, Columbia, and Ecuador.

The mountains were formed when two of the Earth's tectonic plates slammed into each other. What happens when you slide your foot into the edge of a rug? Your foot pushes the rug, and the material scrunches together. This is similar to what happens when two tectonic plates run into each other—only it takes much longer. In South America, two plates in the Pacific Ocean—the Nazca plate and the Antarctic plate—slipped under the South American plate, and this is how the Andes formed. But that's not all! Have you ever rubbed your hands together to keep them warm? Tectonic plates also create heat when one slips under the other. In the Andes, they created so much heat that part of the earth's crust melted, allowing liquid magma to make its way to the surface. The result? Volcanic eruptions!

The climate and plants and animals in the Andes vary depending on where you are, such as how close you are to the Pacific Ocean and how high above sea level you are. Animals such as alpaca, llama, and chinchillas are found in the Andes. Hummingbirds, quetzals, and toucans are birds that inhabit the trees and forests of the area. The Andes have dense deciduous forests, rainforests, and high mountain peaks with little vegetation.

Fun Fact

South American Volcanoes

The volcanoes in the Andes are still active today. Cotopaxi is a volcano found in the Andes in the country of Ecuador. It is currently one of the most active volcanoes in the world.

Island Hopping

The Galapagos Islands are actually peaks of underwater volcanoes that have risen from the sea. There are nineteen islands in the archipelago. Can you see what appears when you connect these nineteen dots?

The Galapagos Islands

The Galapagos Islands are an archipelago along the equator. These volcanic islands are home to some of the world's most amazing animal species. In 1835, Charles Darwin traveled to the Galapagos and found animals unlike any he had seen anywhere else. The animals were familiar—there were tortoises, iguanas, and finches—but they looked different from the animals he was used to. The tortoises were the largest he had ever seen. Some of the iguanas could swim. Darwin didn't even recognize some of the finches because they looked so different. Eventually, Darwin came up with a theory to explain why the animals were different. He wrote that because the animals on the island were so far away from all other living creatures, they had evolved to adapt to their environment. For example, the finches had all developed different beaks so they could eat different types of food without competing with each other.

Because there were no native humans on the Galapagos, Darwin noticed the animals there were not afraid of him. He wrote about picking up an iguana and throwing it into the water, only to watch it rush right back to shore. Darwin picked the iguana up and hurled it back into the water, and the same thing happened. No matter how many times Darwin repeated the process, the iguana insisted on returning to dry land as quickly as possible. Darwin theorized that the iguana's instincts probably told it to get out of the water as quickly as possible to get away from sharks and other predators. The iguana didn't know what Darwin was and didn't see him as a threat, so it returned to land, where it had always been safe before.

The EVERYTHING KIDS' Geography Book

The Galapagos Islands are now a site for ecotourism. Ecotourism is a chance for average people, not just scientists, to travel to parts of the world that have unique and amazing animal and plant life. The goal of ecotourism is to teach people of the beauty of the natural world and to encourage them to protect these important areas of our planet. Protecting and conserving the wildlife and plants in areas such as the Galapagos is important for our understanding of nature and important for the future of our planet!

Let's Visit the Amazon Rainforest

The Amazon Rainforest covers part of nine South American countries. It makes up parts of Brazil, Peru, Guyana, Columbia, Ecuador, Venezuela, Bolivia, Suriname, and French Guiana. Nearly 60 percent of the rainforest is found in Brazil.

What Is a Rainforest?

The Amazon Rainforest is a tropical rainforest. These are located primarily along the equator. On average a tropical rainforest receives between 69 and 79 inches of rain in a year. More than half of all animals and plants on Earth call rainforests their home. Many modern medicines were discovered in these regions or are made of products from the rainforest. The area at the bottom of the tall trees of a rainforest may be called a jungle.

Animals such as the vampire bat, anaconda, jaguar, and leaf cutter ant make their home in the Amazon Rainforest. It is estimated that in a four-square-mile spot in the rainforest, you would find the following:

- 125 different mammals
- 400 different birds
- 100 different reptiles
- 60 different amphibians
- 150 different butterflies

Fun Fact

Harriet the Tortoise

Harriet the Galapagos tortoise died in 2007 at the age of 175. She was living in a zoo in Australia at the time. It is believed that she was actually collected by Charles Darwin in the 1800s on one of his trips to the islands. Imagine the stories she could have told if she could have talked!

One scientist actually studied one small area and found 50 different species of ants alone!

Fauna in the Amazon

No less amazing are the plants that live in the Amazon. The trees and plants in the Amazon Rainforest are very close together and often very tall. They are all reaching to the sky to compete for the sunlight. This area of high treetops is called the canopy of the forest. Some estimate that there may be hundreds of species of birds and other animals living in the canopy that have yet to be identified. Scientists say that if you were to count the trees and plants in 2.5 acres of the rainforest you would find 700 different kinds of trees and maybe 1,400 different types of plants.

The Amazon and Your Climate at Home

Believe it or not, the climate you experience in your area is influenced by the Amazon Rainforest. The Amazon acts like a huge air conditioner for the world. It helps keep the temperatures down a few degrees throughout the world and also balances the humidity and moisture levels in other places on Earth. The trees breathe carbon dioxide, one of the main greenhouse gases. If the trees weren't around to drink up that carbon dioxide, the result would be more carbon in the air heating the entire planet.

Fun Fact

Kapok Tree

The kapok tree is the largest tree in the Amazon. It can reach heights of 200 feet and can be up to eleven feet in diameter. These trees are home to many different insects and birds. The kapok tree has beautiful flowers that attract bats from all over the forest.

DEPARTURES
< gates 4,5,6

pass

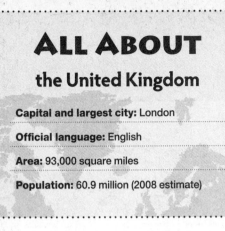

Fun Fact

What Are They Called?

What should you call someone from the United Kingdom? Most people refer to them as being British. But you might also hear people calling themselves Scots, Welsh, Irish, or English. This is because they come from different parts of the United Kingdom—Scotland, Wales, Northern Ireland, or England.

The United Kingdom: Just Across the Pond

The United Kingdom of Great Britain and Northern Ireland consists of four different kingdoms that are sometimes listed as individual countries. England, Scotland, Wales, and Northern Ireland together make up what we can call the United Kingdom.

Great Britain is the largest island in Europe and the eighth-largest island in the world. It's also the third most populous island in the world. There are many natural harbors on the island, and this made travel from the European continent easy. Ireland is separated from Great Britain by the Irish Sea. Northern Ireland is still part of Great Britain, but the country of Ireland, which makes up the rest of the island, gained its independence in 1922. Great Britain is separated from France in the south by the English Channel and from Scandinavia on the east by the North Sea. The channel is so narrow that on clear days, you can stand in the French city of Calais and see the white cliffs of Dover in England. These cliffs reach about 300 feet above the channel, and they are made of chalk, which gives them their unique white color.

England makes up the southern part of the island of Great Britain, and Wales is a smaller area in the west. Most of Great Britain is flat or hilly. The Scottish highlands in the northern part of the island include Ben Nevis, the tallest mountain in the United Kingdom. The terrain and colder climate make it more difficult for people to live there, and it is one of the least populated areas of the country.

The United Kingdom is a rainy place. Along the western part of Scotland, it can rain as many as 250 days in a year! That is nearly seven months of rain—better bring your umbrella!

Pure Europe

Europe is made up of many countries and many peoples. When you mix things up, you can get some very interesting results. Just like the word EUROPEAN.

Fashion and Football

This is the shape of which country in Europe?

How many words can you spell from these letters?

EUROPEAN

Letters can only be used once per word and words must be 3 letters or longer.
Have fun!

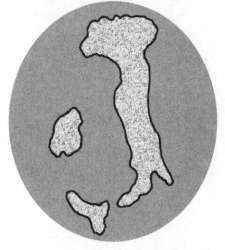

The Loch Ness Monster

Some people think the infamous Loch Ness monster lives in Scotland. What do you think? Is Nessie real? Do some research and use facts and data to try to convince someone of your opinion.

WORDS to KNOW

TUNDRA: The tundra is a very cold and very dry region. These areas are very cold but can be as dry as a desert. The soil in a tundra stays frozen for most of the year. This is called permafrost. Insects, birds, and caribou all live in the tundra.

Fun Fact

Archaeologists think humans came to Europe between 850,000 B.C.E. and 700,000 B.C.E., and they have even found a fossilized footprint on a beach in France that someone left 400,000 years ago.

The United Kingdom has the fifth-largest economy in the world. London is one of the world's major centers of business and finance. The country exports oil and natural gas from its resources in the North Sea.

Mainland Western Europe

There are many countries in Europe. In this book we will split them into three different regions: Western Europe, Eastern Europe, and the Mediterranean region. Let's start by looking at the countries of Western Europe. These countries are typically near the coast of the Atlantic Ocean.

Climate and Terrain

Western Europe has extremes in temperatures, climates, peoples, and cultures. The reaches of Norway and Sweden are covered in frozen tundra. Countries such as Portugal and Spain have beautiful, warm beaches along the shores of the Mediterranean Sea. Many of the other countries of Western Europe are covered by the Alps, one of the major mountain ranges in Europe. France and Spain are separated by the Pyrenees Mountains.

The tiny country of Monaco, which takes up less than one square mile, has a higher population density than any other country in the whole world. There are 32,543 people who call the country home, and they all live in an area that's roughly the size of Central Park in New York City! Compare that with the population density of Iceland, another Western European country. Iceland has only 7 people per square mile.

Fjord Alert!

Western Europe is dotted with fjords. A fjord is a steep, narrow valley carved out of rocks by glaciers. In most cases, a fjord is found near the inlet of a larger body of water. Most fjords reach deeper than sea level. Fjords are found in Ireland, Norway, Sweden, and

Iceland. The Sognefjord in Norway is one of the world's largest fjords. It reaches more than 120 miles inland from the Atlantic Ocean and plunges to depths of close to 4,200 feet below sea level!

The rise and fall of the tides in a fjord are quite dramatic. Because of the high, steep walls and the fact that much of the fjord extends below sea level, the difference between high and low tides can be extreme. When the tide rises in the ocean connected to the fjord, the water rushes into the relatively small fjord. It is best to be prepared for this twice-daily event!

The Great European Plain

The Great European Plain takes up more than 2,400 miles in the interior of the continent. It goes from the Atlantic Ocean in the west to the Ural Mountains in the east, stretching through both Western and Eastern Europe. The plains are generally very flat but are interrupted by hilly forests in Germany.

The Alps

The Alps are one of the major mountain ranges in Europe. The Alps stretch from Austria to Italy and Switzerland and into France. The highest peak in the Alps is Mont Blanc. Mont Blanc (which means "white mountain") is between France and Italy. It reaches more than 15,800 feet into the sky. This makes it the eleventh-tallest mountain the whole world.

The mountains of the Alps were carved by glaciers. These giant ice sheets carved out large basins in the mountains, changed river valleys, and smoothed the rocks there. You can still find mountain glaciers in some of the higher peaks in the Alps. The Alps are a popular tourist destination. In the summer, people enjoy hiking, climbing, and mountain biking. Popular winter sports include skiing, snowboarding, and ice skating. Would you like to visit the Alps? When would you go?

ALL ABOUT
the Countries
of Western Europe

Country	Capital City
Andorra	Andorra la Vella
Austria	Vienna
Belgium	Brussels
Denmark	Copenhagen
Finland	Helsinki
France	Paris
Germany	Berlin
Iceland	Reykjavik
Ireland	Dublin
Liechtenstein	Vaduz
Luxembourg	Luxembourg
Malta	Valletta
Monaco	Monaco
Netherlands	Amsterdam
Norway	Oslo
Portugal	Lisbon
San Marino	San Marino
Spain	Madrid
Sweden	Stockholm
Switzerland	Berne

Hills and Valleys

If you ever go hiking in Europe, knowing another language is a big help. Here are some geographic features in different languages—can you match them with their English name?

Beach	Granica (Polish)
Mountain	Berg (German)
Bay	Vulkaan (Dutch)
Border	Baia (Portuguese)
Desert	Plage (French)
Volcano	Valle (Italian)
Valley	Desierto (Spanish)

Tectonic Talk

What did one mountain say to the other?

I'll meet you in the valley!

The EVERYTHING KIDS Geography Book

Eastern Europe

The landscape, boundaries, and names of the countries of Eastern Europe have changed drastically in the past few decades. It is a unique region rich in culture and tradition. Let's take a look at some of the different regions of Eastern Europe.

A Land of Peninsulas

The easiest European peninsula to spot is shaped like a boot—Italy. However, Eastern Europe has several peninsulas that are all important to the geography of the region. The Balkan Peninsula juts out into the Mediterranean Sea. The Crimean and the Caucasus peninsulas are surrounded by the Black Sea. Shipping and trade by water has always been important to these peninsulas.

Poland

During the Ice Age, glaciers crept as far south as the Polish city of Krakow. Poland is dotted with mountains, rivers, and lakes. In fact, it is one of the countries in the world with the most lakes; it is home to more than 10,000 lakes. There are more than twenty mountains in Poland that reach higher than 6,500 feet above sea level. The highest peak in Poland is Rysys, which reaches more than 8,000 feet into the air. Compare this to Poland's lowest point, which is seven feet below sea level. Poland's land is actually mostly flat except for the mountains in the southern part of the country. The Tatras Mountains in Poland are the highest part of the Carpathian Mountain range that stretches through Eastern Europe from the Czech Republic to Serbia.

Moldova

Moldova is surrounded by the counties of Romania and Ukraine. Most of the country lies between two rivers. These are the Dniester and the Prut rivers. The

ALL ABOUT
Eastern Europe

Albania	Tirana
Armenia	Yerevan
Azerbaijan	Baku
Belarus	Minsk
Bosnia and Herzegovina	Sarajevo
Bulgaria	Sofia
Croatia	Zagreb
Czech Republic	Prague
Estonia	Tallinn
Georgia	Tbilisi
Hungary	Budapest
Kosovo	Pristina
Latvia	Riga
Lithuania	Vilnius
Macedonia	Skopje
Moldova	Chisinau
Montenegro	Podgorica
Poland	Warsaw
Romania	Bucharest
Russia	Moscow
Slovakia	Bratislava
Slovenia	Ljubljana
Ukraine	Kiev

WORDS to KNOW

BOG: A bog is an area that is not well drained. It tends to be marshy and wet and has a lot of plant material. Bogs have their own unique plant life including sedges and heaths.

rivers bring fertile soil to the area. Moldova is one of Eastern Europe's most prosperous farming countries. The people of Moldova raise and export many different fruits and vegetables. People may be most familiar with Moldova for its vineyards—the wine industry in Moldova is quite large.

Estonia

Estonia is in the northern part of Eastern Europe. It is located on the Baltic Sea. The Baltic Sea is an inland sea in Northern Europe. Because of its high latitude, a large portion of the Baltic Sea is covered by sea ice for parts of the year. The Baltic Sea may be murky, but it is not nearly as salty as the ocean.

The land is fairly flat in Estonia. The average elevation above sea level is about 160 feet. The highest point reaches just over 1,000 feet. There are many lakes in Estonia. In fact, one count puts the number of lakes in this small country to be about 1,400. Estonia has many bogs and inlets along its shores.

Estonia is a chilly, rainy place where it can rain as many as 190 days out of the year. The average daily temperature in Estonia is a brisk 41 degrees. The coldest month, February, averages 23 degrees, and Estonia's warmest month is July. The average temperature in July is about 64 degrees. This is the sort of climate you get when you are close the Baltic Sea and influenced by the waters of the Atlantic Ocean and the Gulf Stream.

The Mediterranean: Ancient Cities, Modern Cultures

The countries of the Mediterranean region were where many of the world's ancient cultures and cities were born. These cities and cultures have grown to be today's modern countries.

Mediterranean Climate

The climate of the Mediterranean region is unique to the rest of Europe. The area surrounding the Mediterranean Sea has hot, dry summers and cool, wet winters. This makes it a great place for growing tress such as pines, cypress, and cork. Mediterranean countries such as Greece are known for growing and producing products such as pine nuts, olives, and cheeses.

Volcanoes

The Mediterranean region is a very active place as a far as volcanoes go. Italy has many volcanoes that have been active in recent history and in the past. In fact, the only active volcanoes on the mainland of Europe are found in Italy. One of the world's most infamous volcanoes, Mount Vesuvius, last erupted in 1944. You may have heard of Mount Vesuvius. This is the same volcano that erupted in the year 79 C.E. and buried the ancient cities of Pompeii and Herculaneum with a thick layer of ash. Pompeii and Herculaneum have been excavated, and scientists and historians have studied the artifacts to learn about life in ancient Italy. Pompeii is one of the top tourist sites in Italy today. You can visit and walk through the old city streets and see the ruins of the old buildings.

Another volcano, Mount Etna, has been very active in recent years. It is located off the coast of the Italian island of Sicily, and it is the most active volcano in Europe. Footage from one of the eruptions was used in *Star Wars: Episode III—Revenge of the Sith*. With the help of computer technology, it served as the background for the final fight between Anakin Skywalker and Obi-Wan Kenobi.

Cyprus

Cyprus is an island nation located in the Mediterranean Sea. It is the third-largest island in the

ALL ABOUT
the Mediterranean Region

Country	Capital
Cyprus	Nicosia
Greece	Athens
Italy	Rome

Fun Fact

Sea or Ocean?

The Mediterranean Sea is actually part of the Atlantic Ocean. It is almost entirely surrounded by land and connects to the rest of the Atlantic by the Strait of Gibraltar. This is the area that separates Spain in Europe from Morocco in Northern Africa.

WHAT IN THE WORLD

Stratovolcano

Mount Vesuvius and Mount Etna are stratovolcanoes. Stratovolcanoes are also known as composite volcanoes. This type of volcano is made of layers of ash, rock, and lava that build up in a steep-sided mountain, which eventually explode. These eruptions are violent and can be very dangerous.

Fun Fact

Mount Olympus

The Mount Olympus in Cyprus is not the Mount Olympus you may have heard about from Greek mythology. That Mount Olympus, the home of Zeus, is located in Greece. Olympus is a popular name for mountains. There are others in Utah, Washington State, and even on Mars!

Mediterranean. Cyprus has a varied past, and it has been influenced by both Greece and Turkey. This is because of its proximity to both of these countries.

Greek mythology says that Aphrodite, the goddess of love and beauty, was born on the island of Cyprus—and what a beautiful place to be born! The lowest spots on the island of Cyprus are its beaches, which are at sea level. The highest mountain on Cyprus is Mount Olympus, which reaches about 6,400 feet into the air.

There are two main mountain ranges on Cyprus. The Pentadactylos are in the north and the Troodos are in the south central part of the island. Between these two mountain ranges is an area of fertile soil. This is where most of the farming occurs.

Cyprus is known for its mineral resources. Copper, pyrite, asbestos, and gypsum are all mined and exported from Cyprus. Cyprus is also known for its tourism and exports of clothing. The country has been a place where traders and explorers have stopped for centuries. Its location between Asia, Africa, and Europe makes the small island nation a good stopping point on many voyages.

The European Union

The European Union is a union of 27 countries, or member states. These countries joined together for political and economic reasons. Who belongs to the European Union and what do they get out of it?

After World War II, some of the Western European countries began to discuss how they could keep another war from devastating the continent. Six countries—Germany, France, Luxembourg, the Netherlands, Belgium, and Italy—first cooperated with each other on economic issues; they believed that by acting together, they could make their countries stronger. Other countries saw that this system worked well, and more and more of them began to join together.

The EVERYTHING KIDS' Geography Book

The European Union we know today was formed in 1993. Each country keeps its own independent government but agrees to work with the other members on important subjects such as agriculture, trade, environmental issues, and many more. Acting as one, the member nations have more power politically, economically, and socially than any of them would have alone. New member nations have joined since 1993. Most recently, Romania and Bulgaria joined the European Union in 2007. Countries that want to join the European Union have to apply, and the member nations have to agree to admit them.

The euro is the currency used by many of the members of the European Union. Each country can make its own design for the backs of the coins (tails, if you're flipping them). The front of the coin is the same for all countries.

ALL ABOUT
the Members of the European Union

Austria	Belgium	Bulgaria
Cyprus	Czech Republic	Denmark
Estonia	Finland	France
Germany	Greece	Hungary
Ireland	Italy	Latvia
Lithuania	Luxembourg	Malta
The Netherlands	Poland	Portugal
Romania	Slovakia	Spain
Sweden	United Kingdom	

Only Opposite

Iceland is famous for many things, but two of them are long cold winters and hot, hot springs. Here are some more opposites— can you match them up?

Full	Under	Rough
Dry	Valley	Wet
Mountain	Shallow	Deep
Solid	Over	Empty
Smooth	Molten	

Alps

The Alps are known for their great skiing. This skier is taking on Mont Blanc, the tallest mountain in Europe. Would you rather try out the downhill skiing or the cross country trails in the Alps?

The EVERYTHING **KIDS**' **Geography Book**

North Africa

Country	Capital
Algeria	Algiers
Egypt	Cairo
Libya	Tripoli
Morocco	Rabat
Tunisia	Tunis

the Arabian Peninsula

Bahrain	Manama
Kuwait	Kuwait City
Oman	Muscat
Qatar	Doha
Saudi Arabia	Riyadh
United Arab Emirates	Abu Dhabi
Yemen	Sana'a

the Mediterranean Region

Israel	Jerusalem
Jordan	Amman
Lebanon	Beirut
Syria	Damascus

Camels, Sand, and Pyramids

What do you think about when you hear the term Middle East? Most people think of oil, sandstorms, and the Great Pyramids of Egypt. These are features of this interesting region of the world, but there is a lot more to the Middle East than that. So grab a bottle of sunscreen, some light clothing, and your passport. We are going to the Middle East!

The Middle East is a region of the world located near and around the Mediterranean Sea. There are different ways to map out the Middle East. In this book, you will look at the Middle East in three different areas. These are the Arabian Peninsula, Northern Africa, and parts of the eastern Mediterranean Sea. Let's take a look at the countries and the people who live here.

There are two other Middle Eastern countries that are not included in the lists above. These are Iran and Iraq. These countries have been in the news a lot lately and you have probably heard of them. They are in a group of their own. The capital of Iran is Tehran and the capital of Iraq is Baghdad.

Who Lives in the Middle East?

Let's take a look at one country in each of the regions listed at the beginning of the chapter. This way you will get a better idea of who lives in the Middle East and what their lives might be like. Keep in mind that every country in the Middle East has its own unique characteristics and people. It would be hard to talk about them all as one group.

Egypt

Egypt is a Middle Eastern country located in Northern Africa. Egypt is the thirty-eighth-largest country in the world and is one of the countries in Africa and the Middle East with the most people. Egypt is a giant desert with a river flowing in the middle of it. Most of

Cave Code

If you can break this code, you can find the secret treasure. Follow the instructions to see which square to push to enter the ancient cave. Be careful you don't push the wrong one, or the cave could cave in!

The key is in the row with a hand next to it.

The key has a sun above or below it.

Going in a straight line, the key is 3 squares away from a bird.

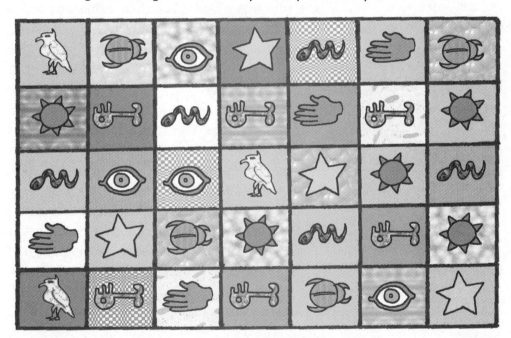

Nature's Storage

Because much of Egypt is dry, artifacts remain in good shape for thousands of years. Caves make a great place for storage because they are also sheltered. In 2004, hundreds of mummies were discovered in caves south of Cairo.

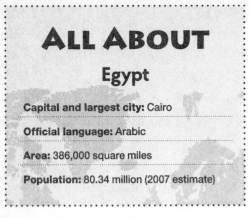

ALL ABOUT

Egypt

Capital and largest city: Cairo

Official language: Arabic

Area: 386,000 square miles

Population: 80.34 million (2007 estimate)

Fun Fact

A New Lake

When the Aswan Dam was built, a new lake formed behind it. When the waters from Lake Nasser are let through the dam, it floods nearly 800,000 acres of land.

the people in Egypt live in cites near this river, the Nile River. They use the river for water, transportation, and industry.

The Nile is the longest river in the world. It is about 4,160 miles long. It starts in Lake Victoria in Burundi and flows northward, emptying into the Mediterranean Sea in Egypt. The area near the Nile is called the Black Land because of the black sediment that was left behind after the floods every year.

The city of Suez in Egypt is home to the Suez Canal, which was built 1869. This canal connects the Mediterranean Sea with the Red Sea. Before the Suez Canal was built, sailors and traders either had to travel around the tip of Africa or cross the deserts on foot or by camel with their goods. This was a long, hard trip and could take many months. The Suez Canal made the trip much shorter and easier.

The Nile River used to flood every year between June and September. This made life for the people along the river dangerous. Finally, people decided something had to be done, and they built the Aswan Dam between 1960 and 1970. It was built to control the floods, not stop them completely. Believe it or not, some flooding is good. When the Nile floods, it helps bring water and fertile soil to areas that need it. However, big floods over a long time can be bad. The Aswan Dam made it possible to control the flooding and release of water. This has helped improve the lives of many people along the Nile.

The dam has helped Egyptians control the floods, but there are other natural disasters the Egyptians can't control. This area has quite a few earthquakes. The rest of Egypt is desert, so drought and sandstorms are common concerns.

Some sandstorms and wind storms remove precious farmland. Oil spills threaten the coral reefs around the shores of Egypt. Wastes and other contaminants pollute the Nile River. The growing population in the regions around the Nile strains the resources there.

Egypt is a beautiful country. Many people travel there every year for vacation. Built 4,617 years ago, the Great Pyramid of Giza is the only one of the Seven Wonders of the Ancient World that is still standing. Scientists and scholars estimate that 590,712 blocks of stone were used to build this pyramid. Some of these blocks could weigh as much as 70 tons, and they had to be moved more than 500 miles from the rock quarries to the site of the pyramid! It is hard to think about what it must have taken to move these blocks, isn't it? It was built as a tomb for the Egyptian pharaoh Khufu.

The people in Egypt work at many different jobs. The fertile area around the Nile produces crops such as cotton, rice, and corn. Farmers raise livestock such as cattle, water buffalo, and goats in this area. People living in the cities have many different jobs. Egypt is known for its textiles. There is oil in Egypt, and many people work to support that industry. Tourism is also a very important part of the economy of Egypt.

Lebanon

Lebanon is a Middle Eastern country that borders the Mediterranean Sea to the west. It borders Syria to the north and east and Israel to the south.

Lebanon has beautiful sandy beaches along the west coast, and the Lebanon Mountains make up the eastern part of the country. On average, the Lebanon Mountains are 7,000 feet tall and are often covered in snow. In fact, the country gets its name from these snow-capped mountains. The Arabic word for Lebanon is *Lubnan*, which means "white" and refers to the mountains. Between the mountains and the Syrian border lies the Bekaa Valley, where most of Lebanon's agricultural products come from. Farmers grow fruits, vegetables, olives, and grapes and raise sheep and goats.

Lebanon has many natural resources. It exports limestone, iron ore, and salt. Have you ever seen the flag of Lebanon? There is a cedar tree in the middle of it. The

Fun Fact

How Great? So Great!

The Great Pyramid of Giza is so large that astronauts can see this awesome structure from the surface of the moon!

ALL ABOUT

Lebanon

Capital and largest city: Beruit

Official language: Arabic

Area: 4,015 square miles

Population: 3.87 million (2006 estimate)

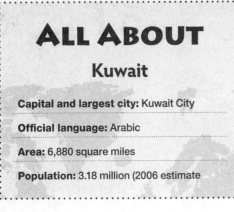

GROSS DOMESTIC PRODUCT: A country's gross domestic product is the amount of money a country makes from the goods (such as oil) and services (such as tourism).

DESALINATION: Desalination is the process by which salt is removed from water. This is used to bring fresh drinking water to people who live in areas with little fresh water. Kuwait and other Middle Eastern countries lead the world in desalination efforts.

cedar trees in Lebanon grow in the Lebanon Mountains in the eastern part of the country. The cedar trees are disappearing, but some still remain. The climate is typical of the Mediterranean—cool, wet winters and hot, dry summers.

Kuwait

Kuwait is a tiny Middle Eastern country located in the Persian Gulf. It's a little smaller than the state of New Jersey, but it is important. It is bordered to the north by Iraq and to the south by Saudi Arabia. The Persian Gulf forms its eastern boundary.

One of the most recognizable structures in Kuwait City is the Kuwait Towers, the premier tourist attraction in this small country. You may have seen pictures of these on the news or in newspapers. They are actually a series of three different towers. The largest has two large globes. The lower globe is home to a revolving restaurant that gives views of the country and the Persian Gulf. The upper, smaller globe is a revolving observation deck. The middle-sized tower can hold up to 1 million gallons of water, and the small tower controls the electricity for the other two. The towers are covered in small plates made of different colored metals. There are 55,000 plates on the towers, all shining in the bright sun to give the towers their shimmery blue color!

There are three main industries in Kuwait. The first is the petroleum industry. Kuwait produces an estimated 2.5 million barrels of oil a day, a large percentage of the oil produced in the world. The oil industry accounts for as much as 60 percent of Kuwait's gross domestic product. Kuwait also has a huge water desalination industry. Taking water from the salty Persian Gulf and processing it to make fresh water is important for the people in this country. The Middle East is a very dry area, and fresh water is very important for people to drink and for farmers to use to grow their crops. Kuwait is also known for its shipbuilding and fishing industries.

Kuwait has faced many environmental problems in recent years. Along with other countries in the Middle East, it is prone to sandstorms, desertification, and droughts. Kuwait also faced a more significant problem. Iraq, Kuwait's neighbor to the north, invaded the small country in 1990. The United States and the United Kingdom led international military efforts to get Iraq out of Kuwait. By the end of February 1991, Iraq had lost the war, but its troops set fire to Kuwait's oil fields as they retreated. As a result, soil and ground water has become contaminated with oil, the air pollution was thick and hazardous, and parts of the southern part of the country have been uninhabitable since then.

Landforms of the Middle East

The Middle East is an area of many hot, dry deserts. But as you will read in this section, there are many bodies of water in the area.

The Tigris and Euphrates Rivers

The Tigris and Euphrates rivers are usually discussed together. The Tigris River is about 1,180 miles long. It has its source in Turkey and then flows south until it meets up with the Euphrates River in Iraq. From there, the two rivers continue as one until they reach the Persian Gulf.

The Euphrates is about 1,700 miles long, and it, too, starts in Turkey. The word "Euphrates" comes from a word meaning fertile. This makes sense as the area around this river would be fertile for growing crops or for livestock. The Euphrates gets its water from the mountains of Turkey, and the river rises when the snow melts every year.

These rivers are home to many different plants and animals. The area is a wetland and has plants such as papyrus. Water buffalo, antelope, gazelle, and jerboa roam this area as well.

Man, It's Dry Here!

Kuwait is a very dry country. In fact, this country is the only country in the world that does not have a natural lake.

OASIS: Have you ever seen a picture of an oasis? These are spots in the middle of a desert with palm trees and water. They are formed by underground springs or rivers. They have been important spots for trade in the desert because that's where people could stop and get water.

Mesopotamia

Mesopotamia is an ancient region of the world. The word *Mesopotamian* means the "land between two rivers." This area is located between the Tigris and Euphrates rivers. Today the countries of Iraq, Iran, Turkey, and Syria are part of Mesopotamia.

Form Features

Two of these are not landforms—
can you tell why?

Cliff

Valley

Canal

River

Bern

Plateau

Plain

Hill

Port

Mountain

Ocean

The Arabian Desert

The Arabian Desert covers most of the Arabian Peninsula. It reaches from Yemen to Jordan. The Arabian Desert has a very dry climate. The most dry area in this desert gets about 1.38 inches of rain in an entire year!

There are not many plants or animals that live here. The temperatures can get pretty extreme, which makes it difficult for life to exist. In the summer the average temperatures are between 104 and 122 degrees. In the winter, the temperatures hover in the forties and fifties but can reach as low as 0 degrees.

Along the border between Saudi Arabia and Oman there is region of quicksand in the Arabian Desert. Quicksand is caused by underground water mixing with the soil. A small amount of water enters into a basin along this border, creating quicksand. Travelers in the desert need to watch out for this hazard.

One of the biggest threats to the Arabian Desert is off-road driving. People take their cars and trucks out into the desert to camp and to drive off-road. This practice, while popular, damages the habitats of the plants and animals that live there.

Did That Gasoline Come from the Middle East?

Did you go to the gas station this week? Chances are pretty good that if you did, the gas you put in your tank came from the Middle East. But the Middle East is known for more than just oil.

The Oil Business

Many countries in the Middle East have petroleum, oil, and natural gas reserves. More than half of the countries in the Organization of the Petroleum Exporting Countries (OPEC) are in the Middle East. OPEC countries have more than two-thirds of the world's petroleum reserves. The OPEC nations meet and decide on things like what price to set for petroleum or how much to drill. As you can imagine, these nations play a big role in our daily lives.

Harvesting for Pearls

Do you know how pearls form? Pearls form when a small bit of sand or shell gets caught inside an oyster. The oyster builds up layers around it until, eventually, a pearl is formed. Pearls are often beautiful and are used in jewelry.

The tiny Middle Eastern nation of Kuwait is one of the world's greatest exporters of pearls. Kuwait does have a large supply of oil, but the pearl industry is also a traditional business in this country.

Tourists in the Middle East

Have you ever seen pictures of the Egyptian pyramids? Countless numbers of people, tourists from around the world, visit the pyramids each year. They come for the sites, to shop in the markets, and maybe ride a camel.

Whew! It's Hot Here! A Look at the Sahara Desert

The Sahara Desert is in Africa and covers most of the countries of North Africa. This desert stretches from the Atlantic Ocean to the west to the Red Sea on the east. It reaches from the Mediterranean Sea in the north to Sudan in the south.

The Sahara is the second-largest desert in the world after the Gobi Desert in Asia. The Sahara is getting bigger. Desertification and climate change are working together to expand the desert. It is believed that the

WORDS to KNOW

WETLAND: Wetlands are also known as marshes or swamps. The soil in a wetland is saturated with water and therefore can only support certain types of plants.

RESERVE: A reserve is a deposit of oil or petroleum that we know about. Reserves of petroleum and oil are found in rocks deep underground. Long ago, plants and other organisms died. Over time the material these organisms left behind changed into petroleum. It takes millions of years to form new reserves.

Papyrus

Papyrus is a tall plant found in the areas surrounding the Nile and the Tigris and Euphrates rivers. These plants can grow to be nine feet tall! Papyrus plants can be cut into thin strips to be used as paper. Ancient people also used them to make boats and mattresses.

Dry Skies

Some people say the Sahara is the world's biggest desert. It covers a third of the African continent, which is about the size of the United States. But according to some definitions, an even bigger desert is Antarctica, which is almost one and a half times bigger.

Whichever you choose, there is very little rain in either place! It looks like these plants could use some rain. Can you see which plant got the most rain? It's in a circle and a square but not a rectangle.

Frozen Funds

Where do penguins keep their money?

In a snow bank!

desert expands southward at the rate of about 18.5 miles a year. This means that many people are losing their fields to the desert and many animals are being displaced.

The Sahara Desert receives the greatest amount of possible sunlight of any place on Earth. The lack of clouds, storms, and pollution mean that this area receives 4,300 hours of sunlight each year. That means it's sunny 97 percent of the time!

The plants and animals of the Sahara are easily recognized. Mammals such as dromedary camels and goats are herded and used for transport, food, or milk. The hyrax, a small relative of the elephant, is found in the Sahara. Most of the plants in this desert are able to withstand droughts and higher than normal levels of salt. Many of these plants have roots that stick deep down into the ground. In some cases, the roots may reach as far down as 80 feet! The roots travel so deep because they are trying to find water. Palm trees, cacti, and acacia trees are well suited for this desert environment.

Fun Fact

Camels

Dromedary camels, which live in Africa, have one hump, and Bactrian camels, which call Asia home, have two. The humps of a camel are used to store fat—not water like many people believe.

Make It "To Go"

Egypt is famous for its mummies. A mummy was buried with many familiar things to provide comfort, both physically and spiritually, in the afterlife. Look for the 16 items hidden in the letter grid.

AMULETS, ANIMALS, BOATS, CLOTHING, FOOD, FURNITURE, GAMES, JEWELRY, MASKS, PERFUME, PETS, POTTERY, SERVANTS, STATUES, TOYS, WEAPONS

```
B O Y R E T T O P W A M U P
S E R V X J E L E W N B X O
B O A T S O S S T Y S O W S
O B A M U L E T S K P A E O
A M U F A Y W S S O O U A E
J E A M X J E A T G T S P M
W G I T L E M R O A T E O U
C N U T U W F U T M O V N F
A I P O M E U S U E X R S R
P H B O A L W A P S U M E E
B T O F U R N I T U R E S P
U O B O K Y N I A M U K Y F
E L T O P D W E A O E S O U
F C Y D T T S E R V A N T S
```

Unexpected Travels

Look on a globe, and you'll find Asia between Europe and the Pacific Ocean. Asia is the largest continent on Earth, with many different people, cultures, languages, religions, and foods. It covers one-third of the planet's total surface, and its population of more than 4 billion people means Asia has about 60 percent of all the people in the world inside its borders. The climate ranges from frozen tundra to steaming jungles, with everything in between and all kinds of wildlife.

The fireworks you watch on Independence Day and the paper in this book are just some of the everyday inventions that came from Asia. Many of the world's main religions originated in Asia. Japanese pottery and fine Chinese and Indian silk are among the most famous crafts from this continent.

There are 50 independent countries in Asia; some of them, such as Turkey, are a part of other regions as well. Since we don't have enough space to look at every country, we'll pick a few well-known ones to visit. We'll also look at the island nations around the Pacific Ring of Fire and the highest and lowest places in this incredible continent. Hang on tight—off we go to Asia!

North Asia

In Chapter 5, you read about Russia in Europe, but Russia is also a part of Asia and the Asian region is called Siberia. Put on your warmest jacket and let's go explore!

With its frozen tundra and dense taiga, you wouldn't think anything could live in Siberia. Yet this area is home to many plants and animals. In the tundra, you can find grass and moss, lemmings, weasels, bears, arctic foxes, and many other animals, as well as dozens of species of birds that fly through here as part of their migration. In the taiga, you can find evergreen trees, reindeer, bears, and squirrels. Close to the border with China, you can catch a glimpse of the famous Siberian tiger, whose fur is thick enough to keep out the bitter cold.

WORDS to KNOW

TAIGA: A taiga is a cold forest that doesn't get much rain or snow. In the summer the ground melts a little bit, but the growing season is very short.

Siberia is also known for its natural resources, such as timber from the taiga, minerals, and crops from the southern steppes—farmlands that yield many kinds of grains. Farmers also raise livestock—cattle, sheep, and reindeer—and run dairy farms.

Known as "blue eye of Siberia," Lake Baikal is the deepest (5,315 feet) and the oldest (25 million years old) lake in the world. It is also home to the world's only freshwater seal, called the nerpa, or Baikal seal.

The people who live in this region have learned to adapt to the cold temperatures. The Yakut people of eastern Siberia get their drinking water in frozen chunks from the local river. They have built their houses up on platforms or wooden stilts to keep them from being damaged by the frost. And they wear lots and lots of clothing to keep themselves warm.

Central Asia

Hidden away high in the Tibetan Highlands, a snow leopard stalks a deer. He moves slowly and carefully, then leaps! Snow leopards are endangered and difficult to spot as they tend to hunt and live alone.

Central Asia is the second-largest region in Asia, and its landscape includes mountains, high plateaus, deserts, and grassy plains. Although most people in this region live in rural villages, working on farms and raising livestock, much of the land is not good for planting and growing food. Some people are nomads, traveling with their livestock and setting up tents wherever their sheep and goats can find food. Then they move on, sometimes visiting a city to sell their products. The sheep and goats provide meat, milk, and wool that is woven into beautiful carpets.

Southwest Asia

Traveling down the continent, we come to the dry deserts of the Arabian Peninsula. You read about many of these nations in Chapter 6, so we'll visit the Republic

---

DID YOU KNOW?

Cross-Country Travel

The Trans-Siberian Railway, built in 1916, is the world's longest continuous rail line. Starting in Moscow at Yaroslavsky Station in the west, it travels 5,778 miles to Vladivostok, in Siberia. The journey takes eight days.

Sputnik I

Kazakhstan became famous in 1957 when it launched the first manmade satellite into space. Then in 1961, Yuri Gagarin, from the city of Baykonur, became the first person in space.

ALL ABOUT
Central Asia

Country	Capital
Kazakhstan	Astana
Kyrgyzstan	Bishkek
Tajikistan	Dushanbe
Turkmenistan	Ashkhabad
Uzbekistan	Tashkent

ALL ABOUT

Southwest Asia

Country	Capital
Afghanistan	Kabul
Armenia	Yerevan
Azerbaijan	Baku
Cyprus	Nicosia
Georgia	Tbilisi
Turkey	Ankara

Turkey

Capital city: Ankara

Largest city: Istanbul

Official language: Turkish

Area: 302,535 square miles

Population: 70.5 million (2007 estimate

Fun Fact

Volcanoes!

Mount Ararat is the largest volcano in Turkey at 16,940 feet. It sits in northeastern Turkey, near Iran and Armenia. Not far away is Little Ararat, at 12,877 feet.

of Turkey, another country like Russia that sits in Asia and Europe. Turkey is surrounded by water on three sides with the Aegean Sea to the west, the Mediterranean Sea to the south, and the Black Sea to the north.

Turkey

Turkey is a peninsula that borders the Mediterranean Sea on the south and the Black Sea on the north. It borders Bulgaria and Greece on the west, and it borders six countries on the east—Georgia, Armenia, Azerbaijan, Iran, Iraq, and Syria. That's a lot of different neighbors!

Turkey's terrain and climate vary greatly throughout the country. Central Turkey can be very dry, but there are other parts of the country that enjoy enough rain to support flourishing forests. Biodiversity is also one of Turkey's main characteristics. During the Ice Age, some animals moved south to present-day Turkey to escape the cold. Some of these species adapted to life in the area and can still be seen there today. Bird-lovers like Turkey because it lies on the migratory routes of many different bird species from Asia, Europe, and even Africa.

Living Dangerously

Most earthquakes and volcanic eruptions occur in the Pacific Ring of Fire,
but millions of people still live along this belt. People live in all kinds of funny places.
Can you figure out where this boy and his cat live? Just connect the dots.

I See You

What city
always cheats
on exams?

Peking

WHAT IN THE WORLD

Rock Houses

In Cappadocia, in the Turkish region of Anatolia, there are very unusual rock structures. Volcanic eruptions millions of years ago dumped lava and ash that eroded into cone-shaped rock towers. People carved the towers into houses, churches, stores, and more. What do you think it would be like to live inside a house like that?

ALL ABOUT

South Asia

Country	Capital
Bangladesh	Dhaka
Bhutan	Thimphu
India	New Delhi
Maldives	Male
Nepal	Kathmandu
Pakistan	Islamabad
Sri Lanka	Colombo

India

Capital city: New Delhi

Largest city: Mumbai

Official language: 18 official languages, including Hindi and English

Area: 1.27 million square miles

Population: 1.12 billion (2007 estimate)

Let's go to the largest city, Istanbul, to see the Sultan Ahmed Mosque. The largest mosque in Turkey, it is known as the Blue Mosque for the blue tiles on its inside walls. It was built between 1609 and 1616, and it is one of the city's biggest tourist attractions. The Blue Mosque is the only mosque in Istanbul with six Muslim prayer towers, called minarets. Istanbul is also unique because it is located in both Europe and Asia. The city is cut in half by the Bosphorus Strait, which connects the Mediterranean and the Black Sea. The part of the city that is west of the strait is in Europe; the part that lies to the east is in Asia.

South Asia

Continuing our travels south, we come to South Asia. This region is one of the most crowded in the world, with 1.75 billion people in an area of 1.73 million square miles. Much of the land is excellent for farming, and there are some cities that have very good economies. However, many more nations are quite poor and their people live hard lives.

South Asia is home to many different kinds of wildlife, from monkeys and mongooses to rhinos, tigers, and elephants. However, the land these animals can live on is getting smaller and smaller as people build more and more homes. Illegal hunting, or poaching, is another problem, especially for the tigers.

India

India is the biggest country in Southeast Asia and the second largest in the world. Look around New Delhi and you'll see colorful saris, smell spicy food, and hear the chatter and noise of a busy city. More than 75 percent of the people in South Asia live in India. These people speak hundreds of different languages, but the main language is Hindi. The three main religions are Hinduism, Buddhism, and Sikhism. Along India's northern border are the mighty Himalayas, the world's tallest range of mountains. The Thar Desert, with its extreme heat, lies to the west. In the south there is lush farmland.

India is located on what's called a subcontinent. It was not originally part of Asia; long ago, it was a piece of land that floated on its own. That changed when it rammed into Asia, creating the Himalayas. They are the tallest mountains in the world, and you'll read more about them later in this chapter.

India has three main seasons—the cool season, the hot season, and the rainy season. During the rainy season, winds called monsoons pass over the Indian Ocean and fill with moisture. Then they blow over the land and let go of the water on the crops below. This season is very important to the farmers in India.

When it comes to food, a typical meal depends entirely on where you live in India. Most Indian people are vegetarians, and Hindus never eat beef because they believe cows are sacred. Most meals have some spicy vegetable dishes, *dal* (lentils), *dahi* (yogurt), and rice or *chappatis* (flat breads). The food is spicy, full of turmeric, chili, cumin, coriander, and cardamom.

Mainland Southeast Asia

Let's travel east and visit tropical Southeast Asia. Its landscape is full of natural resources, such as forests, minerals, fertile soil, and rivers brimming with fish. Most people in this region live in small villages and work as farmers, using traditional methods rather than machinery to work their land. The main crop and food in this region is rice, grown in flooded fields called paddies.

In the big cities, motorcycles, bicycles, and minibuses roar by in the busy streets. Buddhist monks in orange robes weave their way through the crowds. Many of the nations in this region are Buddhist, which means their people follow the words of Buddha, a great teacher who lived in India during the fifth century B.C.E.

DID YOU KNOW?

Saris

A sari is a piece of cloth, about five yards long, that is wrapped around the body so that it looks like a long dress. The loose end is wrapped around a shoulder or around the head. Women often wear a sari with a blouse as well.

Fun Fact

The Taj Mahal

The Taj Mahal, in the city of Agra, was built in the seventeenth century by Shah Jahan, a Mughal emperor. The shah built the structure in white marble as a tomb for his wife. It is a beautiful model of Islamic architecture and a popular site for tourists.

WHAT IN THE WORLD

Angkor Wat

The largest religious temple in the world is in Cambodia. Built in the twelfth century to honor the Hindu god Vishnu, Angkor Wat was also used as an astronomical observatory.

ALL ABOUT
Mainland Southeast Asia

Country	Capital
Cambodia	Phnom Penh
Laos	Vientiane
Myanmar	Yangon
Thailand	Bangkok
Vietnam	Hanoi

Thailand

Capital and largest city: Bangkok

Official language: Thai

Area: 198,114 square miles

Population: 65.28 million (2006 estimate)

Thailand

Let's take a closer look at the nation of Thailand. If you look at Thailand on a map, it looks a little bit like an elephant's head if you use your imagination. It has two big ears that stick out to the sides and a long trunk that stretches into the sea. This is fitting because elephants are the national symbol of Thailand, although there are less than 2,000 elephants left in the wild in Thailand.

Thailand's terrain is very diverse. Coastal Thailand has some of the most beautiful beaches in the world, and fishing is a strong industry. There are rainforests and wet rice fields in the central part of the country. About 40 percent of working people in Thailand make their living as farmers, and many of them grow rice. As you travel north, the land gets drier and more mountainous. Like India, Thailand experiences a rainy season with lots of monsoons.

Journey to East Asia

Mountains, deserts, vast plains, and river valleys cover the landscape of East Asia. China is by far the biggest country in this region, with 85 percent of the area's population and 90 percent of the land area. The Chinese have influenced much of the region's art, writing systems, and languages.

China

With states and cultures going back as far as 6,000 years, China has one of the world's oldest civilizations and the longest continuously used system of writing in the world. Unlike many Western languages, which have an alphabet of 26 letters, the written Chinese language has about 50,000 characters. Each character represents a different word or idea. Japan and Korea both have writing systems that use Chinese characters. The Japanese system is called kanji, and the Korean system is called hanja.

The EVERYTHING KIDS' Geography Book

China is the third-largest nation in the world in terms of land area, and it has the world's largest population. It shares a border with 15 countries, and its climate ranges from tropical in the southern parts to subarctic in the north.

Most Chinese people live in the eastern region of the country, where there are forests, grasslands, valleys, and fertile land where the Yangtze and Huang He rivers wind their way toward the ocean. In the central region you might be able to see a panda way up in the mountains, but there are not many living in the wild anymore.

On the fifth day of the fifth month of the Chinese calendar, the Chinese celebrate a holiday called Duanwu. In English, it is called the Dragon Boat Festival. Celebrating the summer solstice, or the longest day of the year, the festivities include eating *zongzi*—large rice dumplings with red bean inside—and racing long boats that often have decorated dragon heads on them. There are people who paddle the boats and other people who play drums to give the paddlers a rhythmic beat. Dragon boat racing is especially popular in Hong Kong, a state of China.

Japan

Japan is made up of thousands of tiny islands and four main islands, called Hokkaido, Honshu, Kyushu, and Shikoku. Most of these islands have mountains, and some have volcanoes. Volcanic eruptions and earthquakes happen often in Japan. Surrounded by the sea, the Japanese people use fish in their cuisine, including sushi, sashimi, and many others.

On the island of Honshu, about 60 miles from Tokyo, you can see a big snow-capped peak. That is Mount Fuji, the highest point in Japan at 12,388 feet. For many Japanese, Mount Fuji is a sacred mountain. Each year, thousands of pilgrims climb the long path around the mountain to visit the Shinto shrine at the top.

Let's visit a Japanese garden. Influenced by the fancy Chinese gardens, the Japanese wanted their gardens to

ALL ABOUT

East Asia

Country	Capital
China	Beijing
Japan	Tokyo
North Korea	Pyongyang
South Korea	Seoul

China

Capital city: Beijing

Largest city: Shanghai

Official language: Standard Mandarin

Area: 3.7 million square miles

Population: 1.32 billion (2007 estimate)

Japan

Capital and largest city: Tokyo

Official language: Japanese

Area: 145,902 square miles

Population: 127.5 million (2007 estimate)

Longest Largest

Adventurous Dave has traveled all over Asia. He even kept records of how far he walked, but now he has to add them all up. Can you see which one of these 5 rivers is the longest?

Lena (Russia) $1000 + 500 + 500 + 500 + 236 = $ _____

Indus (Pakistan and India) $100 + 900 + 500 + 400 + 76 = $ _____

Yellow (China) $1000 + 1000 + 1000 + 397 + 1 = $ _____

Yangtze (China) $1000 + 500 + 2000 + 417 = $ _____

Volga (Russia) $500 + 500 + 500 + 500 + 266 = $ _____

Pee-Yew!

As well as being the longest river in Asia, the Yangtze River is often referred to as the dirtiest. It is believed that 90 percent of the water in the river is polluted.

The EVERYTHING KIDS Geography Book

fit in small spaces, since Japan is a much smaller country. Most Japanese gardens have these main elements: water, rocks, a stone lantern, a teahouse, a fence or wall, and a bridge to an island or stepping stones. These elements are meant to represent the natural world. Sometimes these gardens are peaceful places for busy people to visit and relax. Sometimes they show off special plants or rocks. Some gardens are meant for the traditional tea ceremony in Japan. And some were once strolling gardens that have become public parks. They are simple and beautiful.

North and South Korea

Korea is located on the Korean Peninsula, with China to the west, the Japanese islands to the east, and Russia to the north. Korea is divided into two independent parts—North and South. The two parts are quite different from one another. North Korea is very restricted—there is little contact with the outside world and the communist government limits the freedoms of its people. South Korea is much more open, trading with the West and producing high-tech products for export. Seoul, the capital of South Korea, has more than 20 million people, making it the world's second-largest metropolitan area behind Tokyo. Seoul has an excellent public transport system, with buses, trains, boats, and planes.

Both North and South Korea are mountainous regions, but North Korea's climate is much more extreme, with very cold temperatures in winter and lots of snow. South Korea has low plains and river valleys that are good for planting rice and soybeans as well as fishing. South Korea's longest river is the Nakton River, which is 325 miles long. It flows from the central mountains to the Korea Strait in the south. The highest mountain, Hallasan, rises 6,398 feet on Cheju Island, just across the Cheju Strait from the southern tip of South Korea.

DID YOU KNOW?

Sun Country

The Japanese call their country *Nippon* or *Nihon*, meaning "source of the sun," which is why Japan is often called "The Land of the Rising Sun."

TRY THIS

Make an Origami Dog

Take a square piece of paper. Fold it in half to make a triangle. Fold it in half again, and then unfold it. With the open end facing down, fold the other two corners down to make the ears. Fold the bottom corner back to make the chin. Draw in a face and give your dog a name!

ALL ABOUT

North Korea

Capital and largest city: Pyongyang

Official language: Korean

Area: 47,918 square miles

Population: 23.5 million (2008 estimate)

The Silk Road

Travel back in time to about 114 B.C.E., during the Han dynasty, and explore the ancient Silk Road that connected East and West Asia through a network of trade routes. People could take goods such as silk, satins, and precious stones along the road from China and Korea to the Mediterranean, selling them in towns along the way or in the big port cities. The introduction of these exotic products helped shape many of the greatest civilizations, such as Persia, Arabia, and Rome. The Silk Road linked China to central Asia, the Middle East, and Europe.

There were several routes that could be taken along the Silk Road. The northern route split into three more routes, two that went around the Taklamakan Desert through present-day Kyrgyzstan, and one that went north of the Tien Shan Mountains through present-day Kazakhstan. Samarkand and Bukhara are two very old cities in Uzbekistan that are famous for their central location along the Silk Road. Some people traveled by sea so their goods would be transported on to Rome and other ports along the Mediterranean. The Silk Road also contributed to the sharing of art, religions, and inventions such as gunpowder, printing, and the compass from the Chinese.

The Islands of Maritime Southeast Asia

Traveling back out toward the islands of Southeast Asia, we come to Borneo, the largest island in Asia and the third largest in the world. It is divided between Indonesia, Malaysia, and Brunei. Borneo is famous for its extensive caves. The world's largest cave is Sarawak Chamber, in Malaysia, at 2,296 feet long.

Off the shores of Indonesia and the Philippines are reefs full of all kinds of coral and ocean animals. These reefs are suffering from illegal fishing, pollution, and global warming. This affects the countries that depend on the reefs for food. There are fewer fish because their habitat is disappearing, which means less food for the fishermen. But demand for the fish is rising because the population in Southeast Asia is always increasing, and the fish are also exported around the world.

The Pacific Ring of Fire

There is an arc of volcanoes that runs through the islands in Southeast Asia called the Pacific Ring of Fire. At 24,855 miles long, it is responsible for 90 percent of the world's earthquakes. It has 452 volcanoes, which make up 75 percent of the world's active and dormant volcanoes. It was created when two of the Earth's tectonic plates collided with each other and one slipped under the other.

In 2004, an underwater earthquake caused a terrible tsunami, or giant wave, in the Indian Ocean. The earthquake had a magnitude of 9.0—so strong that it actually caused the entire earth to shudder slightly. Waves rippled out from the center of the earthquake, gathering speed and strength until they slammed into land.

Unfortunately, there was no warning, and the huge waves devastated coastal villages in Indonesia, Sri Lanka, India, and Thailand. An estimated 150,000 people were killed in 11 different countries. The tsunami caused destruction as far away as Africa.

Way up High and Way down Low

We have traveled all around this incredible continent and seen all kinds of cultures and landscapes. But now it's time to look at the most extreme high and low of Asia—Mount Everest and the Mariana Trench.

Nothing but Sky

Amid the snowy Himalayas, Mount Everest, the tallest mountain in the world, stands majestically in the

ALL ABOUT
Maritime Southeast Asia

Country	Capital
Brunei	Bandar Seri Begawan
East Timor	Dili
Indonesia	Jakarta
Malaysia	Kuala Lumpur
The Philippines	Manila
Singapore	Singapore

Fun Fact

Tsunami in Paradise

Hawaii has been hit by tsunamis twice in the last hundred years, in 1946 and 1960, killing a total of 221 people. Both tsunamis were caused by underwater earthquakes in Alaska's Aleutian Islands. Today, there is a warning system that tells people a tsunami may be coming.

Name That Country!

Land of the Rising Sun is a term often used to describe Japan. Can you match these descriptions for other countries around the world?

Emerald Isle

Land of the Free, Home of the Brave

The Sleeping Giant

Land of the Long White Cloud

The Great White North

Land of the Midnight Sun

Down Under

Land of the Thunder Dragon

South Korea

Australia

Ireland

United States

China

Canada

New Zealand

Iceland

area known as "the Roof of the World." It is 29,029 feet above sea level, and it's still growing at a very slow pace. This gigantic peak was formed when the continents shifted 60 million years ago, moving two land masses together and forcing mountain ranges up into the sky. It is located on the border of Nepal and Tibet.

Climbers flock from all over the world to try to reach the summit. Though Everest is not technically a difficult climb, there are many dangers such as altitude sickness, cold weather, and biting, harsh winds. Avalanches can happen without warning, burying a climber in snow and ice. Mountain climbers are a big source of income for the country of Nepal. The Nepalese government requires that climbers get an expensive permit to climb the mountain. This is to prevent someone from attempting to climb it without proper training. In addition, climbers need guides to help them reach the summit. Sherpas live in the most mountainous region of Nepal and are very comfortable with mountain climbing. They are famous for their strength and endurance at high altitudes. The most famous Sherpa is Tenzing Norgay. He climbed Mount Everest with Britain's Sir Edmund Hillary in 1953. They were the first people to reach Everest's summit.

Hold Your Breath

Dive into the blue Pacific Ocean and head down, down, down to the Mariana Trench—the deepest part of the Earth's oceans. Its lowest point, called "the Challenger Deep" for the British exploration ship HMS *Challenger II,* is 6.9 miles down, and it is located near the Mariana Islands, by the country of Guam.

The EVERYTHING KIDS' Geography Book

To give you an idea of how deep the trench is, you could fit Mount Everest inside it and still have water on top! Once again, this impressive geographic feature is the result of plate tectonics. It marks the point where the Pacific plate slips beneath the Philippine plate.

Can anything live this deep in the ocean? You bet! Tiny little creatures known as microbes, shrimp, crabs, and more love the deep, dark water. Angler fish love the dark. They wave an antenna with a little light on the end to attract their food.

WORDS to KNOW

ALTITUDE SICKNESS: When you go more than 8,000 feet above sea level, you can suffer from altitude sickness. Symptoms include a headache, vomiting, dizziness, and extreme exhaustion. Usually these symptoms go away in one or two days, but sometimes they can get worse. Then you need to go to the hospital!

Lucky House

In China, having a dragon in your home is good luck. A dragon represents abundance and good fortune. Chinese people say they are lung tik chuan ren, which means "descendents of the dragon." How many dragons can you see decorating this lucky home?

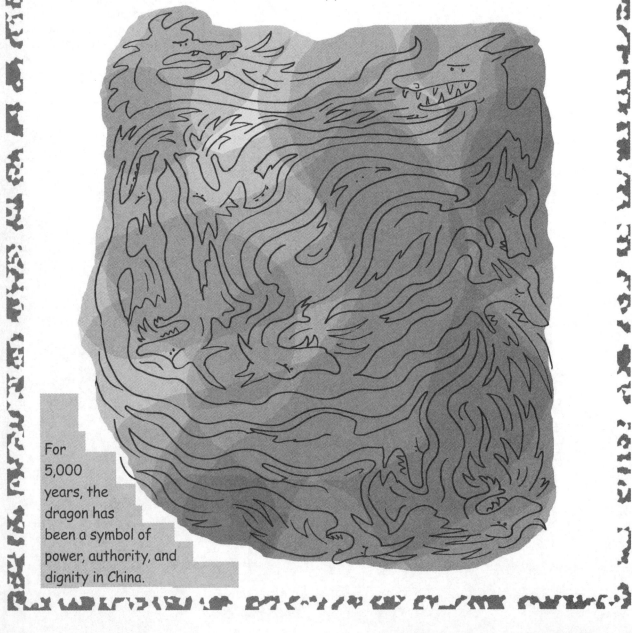

For 5,000 years, the dragon has been a symbol of power, authority, and dignity in China.

The EVERYTHING KIDS' Geography Book

Welcome to the Continent of Africa!

Africa is the second-largest continent in the world. Its landscape ranges from vast deserts to dense rainforests, from grassy savannas to snowy mountain ranges. Africa is home to many of the biggest and best-known wild animals on Earth—lions, zebras, giraffes, crocodiles, hippopotamuses, chimpanzees, gorillas, lemurs, and more. In this chapter, we'll explore the various regions of this historic continent, meet the people who live here, hop over to Madagascar, take a look at the Cape of Good Hope and South Africa, and go on a safari. Bring your binoculars and sunglasses—let's travel to Africa!

Africa is bordered by the Atlantic Ocean on the west and the Indian Ocean on the east, the Mediterranean Sea to the north, and the Suez Canal and the Red Sea to the northeast. Africa is considered to be the oldest inhabited area on Earth. In the middle of the 1900s, anthropologists found fossils and artifacts on this continent that showed human life at least 7 million years ago.

Most of the people in Africa live in rural villages as farmers or herders, but about 20 percent now live in towns. The busiest towns are in northern Africa, especially in Cairo, Egypt, which has about 10 million people. About 775 million people live in a region south of the Sahara called sub-Saharan Africa. More than half of the African population is age 25 or younger because of recent increases in population. The number of babies being born has increased and families are often very large.

There are more than a thousand languages spoken in Africa. While most of them are African dialects, some are Western languages that were introduced by the European countries that ruled in Africa for hundreds of years. And it's not unusual for people to speak several African dialects and also some European languages. You might think all these different languages would make

WORDS to KNOW

ANTHROPOLOGIST: An anthropologist is someone who studies human beings—where they came from and how they lived long ago.

it difficult for people to communicate. It does! But some languages, such as Arabic, Swahili, and Hausa, are spoken by a lot of people, so usually people can find a way to communicate.

There are several hundred ethnic groups in Africa, each with its own dialect and culture. Many groups are split across multiple countries, because border lines were created without considering ethnic unity. Some of the largest groups are the Igbo and Yoruba of west and central Africa, the Kikuyu of eastern Africa, and the Zulu of southern Africa.

Northwestern Africa

The northwestern region of Africa is ideal for farming with its moderate climate along the coast. Warm, wet winters and hot, dry summers are perfect for crops such as citrus fruits, tomatoes, olives, and dates. Further inland is the Sahara Desert. Despite its burning sands and rocks, animals have managed to find a way to live here, and we'll take a look at them toward the end of this chapter. The majority of the people in this area are originally from the Middle East. They speak Arabic and practice the religion of Islam. Many of the buildings in this region look similar to the buildings in the Middle East.

Let's visit Morocco. The full Arabic name for Morocco is Al-Mamlaka al-Maghribiya, which means "the Western Kingdom." Stand in the outdoor *souk*, or market, in Marrakech, a busy city in Morocco. The air is full of the smell of olives and spices. Brightly colored fruits line the stalls. Nearby there is a café serving sweet mint tea. Above the market you can see the snow-capped Atlas Mountains that run through Morocco. Marrakech has the largest *souk* in Africa. The largest Islamic temple in Marrakech is the Koutoubia Mosque, with a minaret that is 221 feet tall. The main industries in Morocco are tourism, agriculture, and chemical production.

WHAT
IN THE WORLD

The Tuareg

Conditions in the Sahara can be extreme. Daytime temperatures can reach up to 122 degrees and at night the temperatures dip below freezing, but there is a tribe called the Tuareg who once traveled huge distances on camels each day to trade their salt. Nowadays, they have settled in the cities in West Africa.

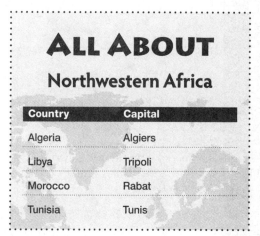

ALL ABOUT
Northwestern Africa

Country	Capital
Algeria	Algiers
Libya	Tripoli
Morocco	Rabat
Tunisia	Tunis

African E-mail

Elise is on safari in Africa. Today she saw elephants and giraffes, so she is e-mailing a picture home to her friends. But it looks like some things got mixed up on the way. Can you see the ten changes in the scenes?

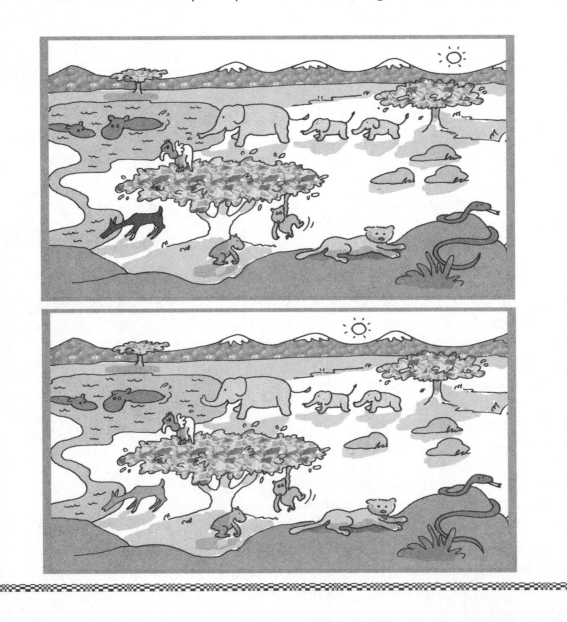

The EVERYTHING KIDS' Geography Book

Northeastern Africa

Traveling east, we come to the countries of Northeastern Africa and the Horn of Africa, so called because it is shaped like an animal's horn. In Chapter 6, you learned that the Nile is the longest river in the world and it flows northward to the Mediterranean Sea. Along the way it flows through Egypt and Sudan, watering the farmlands and giving fresh water for drinking. The Nile is formed by two rivers called the White Nile and the Blue Nile, which meet at Khartoum in Sudan. The Nile is also a big tourist attraction. Cruise ships and traditional sailing boats called *feluccas* carry people down the river to visit the old parts of Egypt.

Let's take our own boat down the Blue Nile to its source at Lake Tana in Ethiopia. The second most populated nation in Africa, Ethiopia is one of the oldest countries in the world. However, it is also one of the poorest because of famine and drought. Farming is the biggest part of Ethiopia's economy, but many farmers grow only enough food to feed their families. The most common crops are coffee, sugar cane, wheat, and corn. Some farmers are herders—people who raise animals such as cattle.

In Ethiopia there is a special way to make coffee. Coffee beans are roasted over hot coals to release oils in the beans. Then they are ground up, put into a clay pot with water, and boiled. The coffee is poured back and forth from one pot into another to cool it. Now the coffee is ready to be served. The coffee is poured from cup to cup without stopping to keep the grounds at the bottom of the pot.

West Africa

Traveling through the Sahara Desert, we come to the varied climate of West Africa. The northern part of this region is an area just below the Sahara called the *Sahel*. The middle regions are grassland and savanna, and

ALL ABOUT
Morocco

Capital: Rabat

Largest city: Casablanca

Official language: Arabic

Area: 172,413 square miles

Population: 33.76 million (2007 estimate)

Northeastern Africa

Country	Capital
Djibouti	Djibouti
Egypt	Cairo
Eritrea	Asmara
Ethiopia	Addis Ababa
Somalia	Mogadishu
Sudan	Khartoum

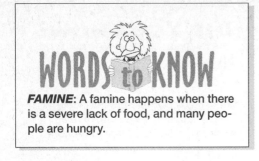

Grocery Store Hunt

The next time you're in a grocery store, go into the coffee aisle and see if you can find coffee from Ethiopia. There are other countries that make and sell coffee. Which ones can you find?

Fun Fact

Story-tellers

In West Africa, history is passed on through stories and music. In Senegal, storytellers called griots go from village to village passing on stories, poems, and songs.

---

the southern region has wet tropical forests. Rainfall increases as you travel south, but overall there is not much rain in this area.

Two kinds of farmers make their living here—those who live on their own land, and those who are nomads, people who move around looking for places where their animals can graze. The nomadic farmers often live toward the north, where land is not good for farming.

Let's get back in our boat and sail along the Niger River to the Republic of Nigeria. This country has more than 250 different ethnic groups. The biggest groups are the Igbo in the east, the Yoruba in the west, and the Hausa-Fulani to the north. Throughout Nigeria there are large areas of land for farming, called plantations, that use machines to harvest and plant. The crops that are grown on these plantations include cotton, coffee, sugar, cocoa, and oil palms. Most Nigerian farmers, however, tend to their own small plots of land, using simple tools to grow food, such as yams, for their families.

Central Africa

Just over the border from Nigeria is the region of Central Africa. Located just above and below the equator, this area is wet and steamy! Rainforests dominate the southern landscape, and it rains all year long. As you move north of the equator, the land dries and turns to grassland. In Chad, the grasslands turn into the hot *Sahel* region.

Let's visit Cameroon, a country with more than 200 different ethnic groups, one of the richest mixes of peoples in Africa. Though Cameroon has had its difficulties, it has prospered from its production of oil and used that money to rebuild the country. Its landscape includes mountains to the west, grasslands to the north, and tropical plains to the south. Similar to many of the other countries we've visited, most of the people in Cameroon are farmers or herders and live in villages or small towns. Some of these people move into the larger urban areas to find better work.

Central East Africa

This region is dominated by the Great Rift Valley, which we will look at more closely in a later section. The valley has broken up the landscape into lakes, narrow canyons, and volcanoes. Elsewhere, a vast savanna is dotted with all kinds of big animals, but the yearly rains in the savanna affect its environment. The grasses in the savannas can grow up to 13 feet tall, sending roots down into the soil to gather moisture. Acacia trees have pointy leaves that won't lose water. Animals wander about the land in search of water.

Crossing over into Kenya, we see a land of riches. Animals are protected in reserves, railroads connect ports and cities, crops such as coffee and tea are exported in great numbers, and tourists flock to see the animals. And yet, many people still only farm their own land, producing enough for their families. Much of the country is not good for farming, so livestock live on that land.

There are more than 42 ethnic communities in Kenya. The Kikuyu are the largest tribe, and they live and farm in the highlands near Mount Kenya. They speak Bantu as well as Swahili and English—the languages of Kenya. The Maasai are a famous ethnic group in this region. They are nomads who travel between Tanzania and Kenya, and their dress and customs are easily recognizable. Their lands include the Serengeti and the Masai Mara National Reserve.

Southern Africa

Travel down through Tanzania and Zambia, and you'll come to the region of Southern Africa, where the Namib and Kalahari deserts dominate the landscape next to tropical forests and grassy plains. Most of the wildlife in this area, such as elephants, leopards, lions, white rhinos, and buffalo, live on the savannas and in the forests. In the Kalahari, the San people, also known as the

ALL ABOUT
West Africa

Country	Capital
Benin	Porto-Novo
Burkina Faso	Ouagadougou
Côte d'Ivoire	Yamoussoukro
The Gambia	Banjul
Ghana	Accra
Guinea	Conakry
Guinea Bissau	Bissau
Liberia	Monrovia
Mali	Bamako
Mauritania	Nouakchott
Niger	Niamey
Nigeria	Abuja
Senegal	Dakar
Sierra Leone	Freetown
Togo	Lomé

Central Africa

Country	Capital
Cameroon	Yaoundé
Central African Republic	Bangui
Chad	N'Djamena
Congo	Brazzaville
Democratic Republic of Congo	Kinshasa
Equatorial Guinea	Malabo
Gabon	Libreville
São Tomé and Príncipe	Sao Tomé

Copy Continent

Africa is a huge continent. Can you tell which two of these upside-down maps are exact copies of the original?

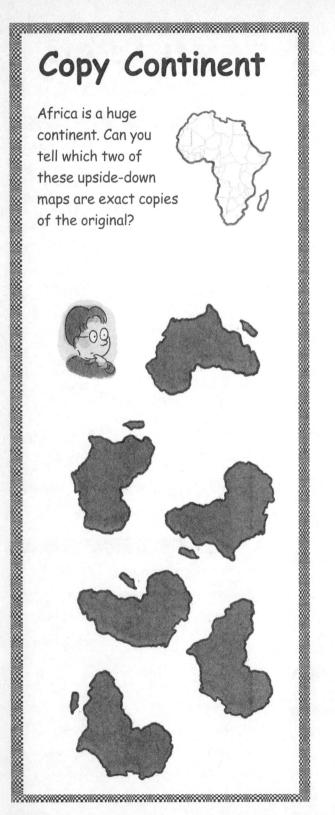

Bushmen, live as hunter-gatherers, using bows and arrows to hunt wild animals and gathering plants and fruits for food. Their language is very unique, with distinctive clicking sounds. Their homes are constructed of natural building materials, such as branches and long grass.

Let's go visit Zimbabwe, a landlocked country bordered by Botswana, Zambia, South Africa, and Mozambique. There are several environmental problems in Zimbabwe. The forests are disappearing, the land is washing away, and there is lots of pollution. In addition, both the black and white rhinos are endangered because of poaching.

Most of the people in Zimbabwe are Shona, a diverse group of tribes who live in the center and east of the country. Most are farmers, but some are starting to work in cities.

The Cape of Good Hope and South Africa

The Cape of Good Hope is a peninsula located a little northwest of the southern tip of Africa, but it is a critical spot for ships that travel around Africa as they enter or leave the Indian Ocean. The first name for the Cape was "Cape of Storms," given by Portuguese explorer Bartolomeu Dias in 1488. It was later renamed "Cape of Good Hope" because it offered a way to access India and the East. Hundreds of large ships sail around the Cape every day. Many are oil tankers leaving the Persian Gulf.

South Africa

Back on the mainland, we arrive in the Republic of South Africa. The South African

The EVERYTHING KIDS' Geography Book

coast is 1,739 miles long, bordering both the Atlantic and Indian Oceans. Cape Town was founded in 1652 by the Dutch East India Company as a rest stop along the way around Africa. South Africa's population is very racially diverse, made up of Caucasians, Indians, and racially mixed communities. The main ethnic groups include the Zulu, Xhosa, Basotho, Bapedi, Venda, Tswana, Tsonga, Swazi, and Ndebele, all of which speak Bantu languages.

South Africa is surrounded on three sides by oceans, and it is located in the mild southern hemisphere, which causes the climate to be mostly temperate. But there are also several climactic zones in this region, from the hot Namib Desert to the subtropical area near the Mozambique border. The southwestern climate has wet winters and hot, dry summers, making it the perfect place to make wine. This area also has very strong winds that make it challenging to sail around the southern tip of Africa. The southeastern coast, on the other hand, is green and lush, giving it the name Garden Route. The wetlands in the Garden Route are visited by hundreds of species of birds.

Fun Fact

Rhinos

Both black and white rhinoceroses are actually gray, but their different lip shapes set them apart and are related to what they eat. The black rhino's upper lip is pointed, because black rhinos use their lips to remove leaves and fruit from trees and bushes. A white rhino's upper lip is more square, because they munch on grass with their heads pointed at the ground.

ALL ABOUT

All about South Africa

Capitals: Pretoria (administrative), Bloemfontein (judicial), Cape Town (legislative)

Largest city: Johannesburg

Official languages: There are 11 official languages.

Area: 470,462 square miles

Population: 47.9 million (2007 estimate)

ALL ABOUT

Madagascar

Capital and largest city: Antananarivo

Official languages: Malagasy, French, English

Area: 228,880 square miles

Population: 20 million (2008 estimate)

Madagascar

We've looked at the countries on the mainland of Africa. Now it's time to travel off shore to Madagascar. It is located near the southeastern coast of Africa, and it is the fourth-largest island in the world. Because of its isolation, Madagascar has many different kinds of plant and animal species that are only found in this country. One of the most famous animals in Madagascar is the lemur, a relative of monkeys. Other animals include chameleons, tortoises, moths, and butterflies. One animal that no longer exists—because it disappeared about 1,000 years ago—is the elephant bird. It could not fly, was about 10 feet tall, and weighed around 1,000 pounds.

With highlands, fertile farmlands, mountains, river valleys, and a desert, Madagascar has a varied landscape. Its climate is warm and moist near the coast but hot and dry in the southern desert. Farming, fishing, and forestry are the main industries, with coffee and vanilla at the top of the list of exports.

Spelling Sailors

It is believed that people from Southeast Asia found a route to Madagascar between 200 A.D. and 500 A.D. These sailors are following a route too, but only one of them works—it has the correct letters to spell Madagascar.

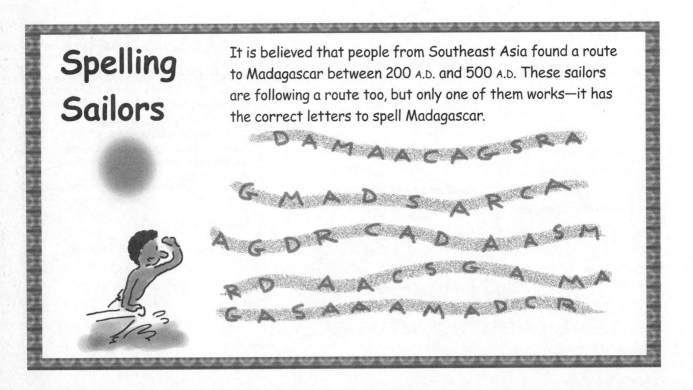

The people who live on Madagascar are called Malagasy. Made up of several ethnic groups, they are a mix of Indonesian and black African descent. The language they speak is also called Malagasy. It is similar to Malay, the language of Malaysia, and Indonesian. French and English are also official languages of Madagascar.

Safari Time!

We've visited countries, seen beautiful landscapes, and met very interesting people, but we haven't seen any big animals yet. Let's go on a safari! There are many national parks and game reserves in Africa, so we're going to visit the Masai Mara National Reserve in Kenya, the Serengeti National Park in Tanzania, and the Bwindi Impenetrable Forest in Uganda.

Serengeti National Park and Masai Mara National Reserve

Let's start at the Serengeti National Park. With 5,700 square miles of savanna, grassland, and forest, this park has many different kinds of animals, including elephants, rhinoceroses, lions, leopards, and buffalo. All of these animals are well suited to life on the savanna because of what they eat and how they roam. We're going to try to spot a lion.

Don't get too close! Lions may be related to cats, but they're much bigger and have much longer teeth. A group of lions is called a pride, and a pride is made up of female lionesses, cubs, and a few adult male lions. The lionesses are the hunters and they work together to bring down an animal for food. The male lion is easy to spot because of his giant mane—the ruff of fur around his face—and he can weigh anywhere from 330 to 500 pounds. A female lion's weight can range from 270 to 400 pounds. Lions eat large animals, such as wildebeests, zebra, and buffalo.

DID YOU KNOW?

Leaping Lemurs

Lemurs are found only on the island of Madagascar and on the nearby Comoros Islands, living in both rainforests and dry deserts. They spend most of their time in the trees. They are very social animals, living together in groups.

FORESTRY: Forestry is the science of developing and caring for forests. This job involves helping forests recover after trees have been cut down for paper and managing the wildlife that lives in the forests, among many other responsibilities.

Fun Fact

Animals of Africa

Did you know a giraffe's tongue can measure up to 21 inches long? The giraffe's long neck lets it reach food on the tops of the acacia trees, and its long tongue helps it get around the trees' thorns so it can eat its favorite food!

Have you ever heard of an animal called the wildebeest? It may be funny-looking but it's extremely important to the ecosystem of this area. Every year in midsummer, visitors to the park are treated to an incredible sight. Millions of wildebeests migrate as a single herd from their winter home in the Serengeti to their summer home in the Masai Mara National Reserve. They travel more than 600 miles, arriving toward the end of summer. These creatures have been migrating this path for millions of years. They know how to follow the rains and the green grass. When the grass is gone, between November and January, they turn around and head back to the Serengeti. This event is called the great wildebeest migration. This region depends on the wildebeest to eat the grass that could catch fire and destroy the land. In return, the wildebeest are food for predators such as lions.

The Masai Mara National Reserve is one of the most famous reserves in Africa because of its wide-open landscape and incredible wildlife. Especially during the wildebeest migration, you can see thousands of animals, including zebra, impala, giraffe, hyenas, leopards, lions, cheetahs, jackals, hippos, and Nile crocodiles.

Bwindi Impenetrable Forest

There are many animals that live outside of the savanna. Let's travel into the Bwindi Impenetrable Forest in Uganda, home to half of the world's population of mountain gorillas. Be very quiet, and you just may see one. These gorillas are endangered, so there aren't many left alive. They live deep in the forest, eating leaves, bark, and fruit. Every night, they build nests to sleep in from the surrounding plants. The adult males are called silverbacks because of the stripe of silver hair on their backs. Normally, mountain gorillas walk on all fours and stay on the ground, but when they stand, they can be up to five or six feet tall.

Surprising Birds

Continuing our trek south, we head to South Africa where we see . . . penguins! There's no snow, and these penguins can't fly, but they can swim very well and very fast. The African penguin, also known as the black-footed penguin, can reach speeds of 12 miles per hour and can hold its breath underwater for up to two minutes. A group of penguins is called a colony.

Sahara

Journeying north, back to the Sahara Desert, we meet an animal called the fennec fox. Its light brown color blends in with the sand, and it eats all kinds of food, from plants to insects, eggs, and rodents. This fox is best known for its unusually large ears, which not only help keep it cool but also allow it to hear tiny

Fun Fact

Wacky Wildebeests

According to an old African legend, the wildebeest was put together by God using spare parts from other animals, which is why it is such a silly-looking animal!

DID YOU KNOW?

Hippos

Adult hippos can stay underwater for up to five minutes. When they sleep, they rise to the surface to take a breath.

insects moving along the sand. Other animals in the Sahara include the Saharan cheetah, dromedary camels, monitor lizards, sand vipers, and ostriches.

The Highest, Coldest, Largest, Deepest, Longest, and Hottest in Africa

Are you ready for an adventure? We're going to visit all the extremes in this incredible continent.

First, we travel to El Azizia in Libya, where the highest temperature ever recorded was 136 degrees. The coldest spot in South Africa is the town of Sutherland, in the western Roggeveld Mountains. Temperatures in winter can go as low as –5 degrees.

Next we go over to Egypt and the Nile, the longest river in the world at 4,132 miles. Heading south to Uganda and Tanzania, we can dive into Lake Victoria, Africa's largest lake at 26,560 square miles and the second-largest freshwater lake in the world. If you stand close enough to Victoria Falls, you can feel the spray from the largest waterfall in Africa, with a total height of 360 feet and a width of 1 mile.

At Tanzania's border with Kenya, we can climb Mount Kilimanjaro, Africa's largest mountain at 19,341 feet. The Drakensberg Mountains are the highest in Southern Africa, rising to a height of 11,422 feet.

That was quite an adventure! But our trip around all the landforms of Africa would not be complete without visiting the Great Rift Valley. Starting in Lebanon and extending south to Mozambique, the Valley is made up of separate valleys and fault lines that include the Rift Valley Lakes, such as Lake Tanganyika. It runs 3,700 miles in length. Scientists have found early human bones and artifacts in its eastern branch, near Kenya and Ethiopia.

CHAPTER 9

Australia

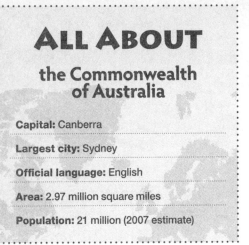

ALL ABOUT
the Commonwealth of Australia

Capital: Canberra

Largest city: Sydney

Official language: English

Area: 2.97 million square miles

Population: 21 million (2007 estimate)

Welcome to the Land Down Under

The continent of Australia is defined in different ways depending on the geographer. In this chapter, we'll include Australia, New Zealand, Papua New Guinea, and all the other Pacific islands in a region called Oceania. We'll hike around these countries, explore their landscapes and wildlife, taste some local cuisine, and more.

Surrounded by the Indian and Pacific Oceans, the Commonwealth of Australia is the smallest of the seven continents but the largest country in the region of Oceania. It is made up of six states: New South Wales, Queensland, South Australia, Tasmania, Victoria, and Western Australia. Two-thirds of the country is covered in scorching hot deserts. Most people, therefore, live along the 21,262 miles of temperate coastline where the weather is mild and wet. The northern part of the country has a more tropical climate, with rainforests and swamps.

The People of Australia

The first people to arrive in Australia were the Australian Aborigines, who got there about 40,000 years ago. Scientists believe they arrived by boat from Southeast Asia. At this time, the islands were closer together, and the seas were not as high. When European settlers arrived in the late 1700s, there may have been 500,000 to 1 million Aborigines living in Australia. This number went down because of disease and war. Today, the Australian government is helping the Aboriginal people, giving them citizenship and the right to own their land.

Not a Baaad Life!

There are about 120 million sheep in Australia, making this country the top producer of wool in the world. The sheep are merinos, brought over from South Africa and England. Their wool is very fine and soft. Farmers use dogs and horses to herd and lead their flocks. Sometimes the flocks can have thousands of sheep on farms called stations. Then farmers use motorcycles and trucks to keep track of the animals. Removing the wool from sheep is called shearing, and the people who do it are called shearers. Mining is another big industry, and Australia is the world's top exporter of coal and diamonds, as well as many other minerals.

Life in Australia

The cuisine in Australia is largely made up of meat—specifically beef, chicken, pork, lamb, and mutton, which is sheep. Because the British claimed part of Australia in the 1700s, their foods influenced Australian cuisine for quite a while. Recently, immigrants from other parts of Europe have come to live in Australia and brought their foods with them, adding even more new dishes to the mix.

Sports are a big deal in Australia, especially cricket, tennis, and a special kind of football called Australian Rules. People also love to swim, surf, and sail in the warm coastal waters.

The Geographical Wonders of Australia

The Australian landscape is amazing and diverse, from the watery beauty of the Great Barrier Reef to the rugged eastern mountains and the dusty outback.

The Great Barrier Reef

Slip on your mask, snorkel, and fins and get ready to dive into the Great Barrier Reef! Located off the northeastern edge of Australia in the Coral Sea, the Barrier Reef is about 1,600 miles long and is made up of nearly 3,000

WHAT
IN THE WORLD

individual reefs. Since coral are living organisms, that makes it the largest structure built by living creatures. It is even longer than the Great Wall of China!

This colorful underwater garden, with more than 400 different kinds of coral, is home to more than 1,500 species of fish, including clownfish, red bass, and coral trout that swim in and out of the nooks and crannies of the reef. Jellyfish, sea anemones, sea urchins, starfish, and other marine animals latch on to the coral. Many animals come to the reef to have their babies, including humpback whales (who swim all the way from Antarctica) and sea turtles. More than 200 species of birds make their nests nearby.

The Great Dividing Range

Extending 2,175 miles, Australia's biggest mountain chain runs from the northeastern edge of Queensland down the eastern coastline to western Victoria. Australian Aboriginal tribes once lived in these mountains, leaving behind their tools as artifacts. When European settlers arrived in the eighteenth and nineteenth centuries, the mountains stood in the way of good farmland. They set out to find paths through the range. Their routes led to new settlements along the coast.

The range, also known as the Eastern Highlands, has parts that are flat and moist, making them good for farming. There are other areas that are steeper, such as the Australian Alps, which include Mount Kosciuszko—Australia's highest mountain at 7,310 feet above sea level.

Hot! Hot! Hot!

As we travel further inland, away from the eastern coast of Australia, the temperature goes up. We are nearing the deserts of the Outback. The largest deserts are the Simpson, the Gibson, the Great Sandy, the Tanami, and the Great Victoria. The combined size of these deserts is about 500,000 square miles.

Add Up Australia

Nearly 20 percent of Australia is considered to be desert. This makes it the second-driest continent in the world (right after Antarctica). Another 15 percent receives so little rain it is almost desert. That's 35 percent of the country—a lot of dry land! Can you add up these amounts to find the answers?

How many deserts are there in Australia

5 + 4 + 2 = _____

The largest rock in the world is Ayers Rock in Australia. How many miles is it around the base?

½ of 10 + ½ of 1 = _____

There's a ranch in Australia called Strangeray Springs that is almost as big as Belgium, making it the largest ranch in the world. That's a lot of cows! How many square kilometers is it?

10,000 + 10,000 + 5000 + 5000 + 29 =

_____

The Great Barrier Reef is the world's largest coral reef system; it is so big, it can be seen from outer space. It is located just off the coast of Queensland, Australia. How many individual reefs make up this system?

500 + 500 + 1000 + 400 + 500 =

_____

The climate here is hot and dry. In fact, Australia gets so little rainfall that it is the driest inhabited continent on Earth. There are not many people who live here, but you can find farmers who raise their livestock in certain places that have plants for food or fertile land for farms.

At the eastern edge of the outback there stands a giant rock formation called Uluru, also known as Ayers Rock. One of the most familiar land formations in Australia, it is almost six miles around and stands 1,142 feet above sea level. Throughout the day, Uluru seems to change color, and at sunset the rock glows bright red. Uluru is made of sandstone, and it is left over from a mountain range that eroded away. This rock is very special to Aboriginal culture.

Snakes, Koalas, Kangaroos, Lizards, and More!

Keep your eyes peeled as you walk around! Australia has an incredible amount of wildlife that cannot be found anywhere else in the world. Let's take a look at some of them.

With the bill and webbed feet of a duck, the body and fur of an otter, and the tail of a beaver, the platypus is one funny-looking animal—but when this animal slips underwater, all its odd parts make it an excellent swimmer. Its webbed feet are perfect for paddling and its tail helps it to change direction. The platypus uses its bill to search for food, because it has to shut its eyes, nose, and ears to keep water out. The platypus can stay underwater for more than a minute. Another amazing thing about the platypus is that, even though it is a mammal, it lays eggs.

What's about seven feet tall, has strong back legs, and can hop faster than 35 miles an hour? You guessed it—the kangaroo. There are more than 70 different kinds of kangaroos. A baby kangaroo, called a joey, is teeny-tiny at birth. He climbs into his mother's pouch and stays there for two months, drinking milk and growing bigger, until one day he sticks his head out and is ready to face the world. A group of kangaroos is called a mob.

Now look up in the eucalyptus trees and you'll see a mother koala and her baby. Most likely, they're asleep. Koalas sleep for up to 18 hours a day! Koalas, like kangaroos, are marsupials, which means the mother has a pouch on her stomach that her baby climbs into after birth. The baby koala stays safe in the pouch for six months. Then she rides around on her mom until she is about one year old. Koalas eat about two-and-a-half pounds of eucalyptus leaves every day.

A third type of marsupial is the wombat. Unlike koalas, however, wombats dig burrows and live underground. These burrows often connect to other burrows, creating a whole neighborhood right under your feet! Wombats are nocturnal, which means they come out at night to look for food such as bark, grasses, and roots. These little guys are pretty fast for their small size—when they're in trouble, they can run up to 25 miles per hour for more than a minute!

Australia has more lizards than anywhere else in the world. There are 114 species of gecko—a small lizard that can climb walls and walk across ceilings. Other lizards include the spiny thorny devil, the frill-necked lizard, and the perentie—a monitor lizard that can grow to be more than six feet long.

Don't look in the sky to find an emu—they can't fly! The largest of Australia's birds, the emu can grow to more than six feet tall and has long legs and short wings. They can run very fast, though, sprinting at speeds of up to 30 miles per hour. Another unusual bird is the kookaburra. Their name refers to the sound they make, which is similar to laughter. They eat snakes, insects, and lizards.

In the outback, you can find all kinds of interesting wildlife, including wild dogs called dingoes, red kangaroos, and wild camels. Many of these animals sleep

Devil in Disguise

Only one of these Tasmanian devils is real; the rest are impostors. Can you see who has sunglasses, short round ears, two sharp teeth, and a black nose?

Is There Really a Tasmanian Devil?

through the hot days and come out in the cooler evenings to find food.

One of Australia's smallest and most familiar states, Tasmania is a small island off the southeastern edge of Australia. It is only 190 miles long, but its landscape and unique animals make it a popular destination for tourists.

The People

The first people to live in Tasmania were the Tasmanian Aborigines, who got there as long as 35,000 years ago. In the early 1800s, Europeans arrived and established the town of Hobart. The settlers were mostly prisoners and their guards, and their responsibility was to set up farms and other industries. Nowadays, most people live in cities on or near the coast, such as Devonport, Launceston, and Hobart.

The Landscape

Tasmania includes a main island and many smaller islands. The landscape changes from flat plateaus that are perfect for farming to rough mountains and river valleys. The climate in Tasmania is temperate, with relatively mild winters and summers. The western region gets lots of rain from winds that cross the Indian Ocean. The east coast of the state is much drier. The highest recorded temperature was 105.4 degrees in Hobart on January 4, 1976. The lowest temperature of 8.6 degrees occurred at Butlers Gorge on June 30, 1983.

Some of the oldest and biggest trees in the world live in Tasmania. In the northwestern

The EVERYTHING KIDS' Geography Book

region on Mount Read, there is a group of trees called the Huon Pines that are more than 10,500 years old. There are Mountain Ash trees in the Styx Valley that can reach heights of more than 300 feet.

The Animals

Tasmania has many different kinds of animals, some of them with very interesting names. Let's find out all about them.

The barred bandicoot is a small marsupial with a large head, a narrow pink nose, large ears, and soft fur with stripes, which give the animal its name. The bandicoot is nocturnal, spending its days in a nest and coming out at dusk to look for beetles, worms, and berries.

The Tasmanian tree skink is a small lizard, about one to two inches long with a pink-orange belly. The skink loves to climb and is often found on trees. It also makes its home under bark and in logs. The tree skink is an unusual reptile. Most reptiles give birth to babies in eggs, but the tree skink gives birth to a live baby.

Have you ever heard of the Tasmanian devil? It is a furry, black marsupial that gets its name from its scary screeches and bad temper. It has a short, wide body about three feet long, strong legs, and a big head and ears. This animal is a scavenger, but sometimes it kills and eats animals, too. The Tasmanian devil is also nocturnal, sleeping during the day in dens or caves.

The Land of the Long White Cloud

If we sail even further southeast of Australia, we can explore the two big islands that make up New Zealand. The Maori name for New Zealand is Aotearoa, which means "the land of the long white cloud." New Zealand is made up of the North Island and the South Island. The North Island is mild and warm. Since it is part of the Pacific Ring of Fire, it has active volcanoes like Mount Ruapehu, which stands 9,177 feet above sea level. The

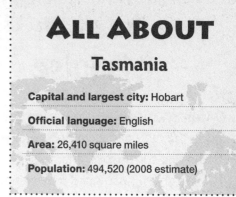

ALL ABOUT
Tasmania

Capital and largest city: Hobart

Official language: English

Area: 26,410 square miles

Population: 494,520 (2008 estimate)

SCAVENGER: A scavenger eats another animal that is already dead, rather than killing and then eating the animal.

ALL ABOUT

All about New Zealand

Capital: Wellington

Largest city: Auckland

Official languages: English, Maori, and New Zealand Sign Language

Area: 103,738 square miles

Population: 4.27 million

Penguins in New Zealand?

It's true—there are two kinds of penguins native to New Zealand. The yellow-eyed penguin is pretty big—about 30 inches long and about 14 pounds. It has a pale yellow head, yellow eyes, and a yellow stripe around its head. The little penguin, also known as the little blue penguin, lives in Australia and New Zealand. These weigh about two pounds and are about 16 inches tall.

South Island is divided by the Southern Alps and has a much colder climate. The highest peak on the South Island is Mount Cook at 12,320 feet. The two islands are separated by the Cook Strait. Because New Zealand is so isolated, many of its plants and animals are unique and can't be found anywhere else in the world.

Sheep, Penguins, and Kiwi

Let's take a look at the landscape of New Zealand. The wet climate is ideal for raising livestock, and, like Australia, New Zealand has lots and lots of sheep—around 45 million, in fact. Not surprisingly, this country is one of the world's top exporters of wool as well as farm products such as butter and cheese. There are also many orchards, in which farmers grow fruits such as citrus, berries, apples, and many others. The farmers sell these fruits to farmers in the Northern Hemisphere when that part of the world is in the middle of winter and cannot grow fruits.

Much of New Zealand's electric power comes from something called a hydroelectric plant, which uses the fast-running water of a river to turn a wheel, called a turbine. The turbine then turns a generator that makes electricity. Clyde Dam, on the South Island, is an example of a hydroelectric plant. Because New Zealand does not have many people, its industries don't make a lot of pollution and it gets its power from rivers, so it is considered an environmentally friendly country.

The most famous symbol of New Zealand is the kiwi—a bird that cannot fly. The kiwi has a very good sense of smell, and it uses the nostrils at the end of its beak to help it find insects and worms underground. The kiwi is also nocturnal, avoiding animals that might eat it during the day. A fuzzy brown fruit, also called a kiwi, is named for the bird.

The **EVERYTHING** KIDS' **Geography Book**

New Zealanders

New Zealand was one of the last countries on Earth to be inhabited. Settlers arrived from Polynesia around 950 C.E. across a land bridge that once existed between New Zealand and Southeast Asia. The Maori are descendants of those original settlers, and they make up 14 percent of the country's current population. The rest of the people in New Zealand are descendants of the European settlers who arrived in the 1800s. The Maori language has been adopted as an official language and Maori culture has greatly influenced New Zealand. Most of the people in present-day New Zealand live in cities, and more than half live in the four biggest cities: Auckland, Wellington, Hamilton, and Christchurch.

Like Australians, New Zealanders love sports—especially hiking, mountain climbing, and rugby. New Zealand's rugby team is called the All Blacks, and they often play Australia's team, the Wallabies.

The Island Nations Surrounding Australia

The Pacific Ocean is the deepest and largest ocean in the world. It covers one-third of the Earth's surface. There are somewhere between 20,000 and 30,000 islands in the Pacific Ocean. Some of these islands are high islands, with volcanic, fertile soil. Others are low islands or reefs, with soil that is not fertile. The people who live on these islands fall into three groups: Melanesians, Micronesians, and Polynesians. Let's take a look at the countries of Papua New Guinea, Fiji, and the Marshall Islands.

Papua New Guinea

The largest Pacific island, New Guinea is a part of Melanesia and contains the country of Papua New Guinea. The population is very small, but it is one of the most multicultural, with more than 850 different native languages and traditional cultures.

Bubble Trouble

A lot of geography results from the movement of tectonic plates, which creates volcanoes, troughs, and lowland basins. Rotorua, New Zealand, is well known for geysers and hot mud pools. These geysers can get very hot and dangerous. It looks like some other dangers lurk here. Can you find nine daggers, four axes, and five spiders?

It's a Gas

What did the daddy volcano say to his son volcano?

I lava you!

The EVERYTHING KIDS' Geography Book

The landscape is varied, with a chain of mountains extending down the island of New Guinea that separates the highly populated rainforest areas from the low, coastal areas that feature swamp forests. The highest peak in Papua New Guinea is Mount Wilhelm at 14,793 feet. There is often snowfall up in these high mountains. The nearby Pacific Ring of Fire causes volcanic eruptions and earthquakes that can lead to tsunamis. Dense forests and rough terrain have kept many of the country's ethnic groups isolated from one another.

Australia, New Guinea, and many other islands are part of an ecological region called Australasia, and many of these countries share similar animals. You can find kangaroos and possums in Papua New Guinea. You can also find the largest butterfly in the world—the Queen Alexandra's birdwing butterfly. Females have a larger wingspan than males—more than 14 inches—and their bodies are around three inches long. Their long wings make them strong fliers, and they like to fly in the early morning and the early evening. There are many birds of paradise here and more kinds of orchids than anywhere else in the world.

The people of Papua New Guinea mostly live on farms and practice subsistence farming, which means they grow enough food for themselves but not enough to sell. Minerals such as oil, copper, and gold are most of the country's exports. Popular foods include wild sago, which comes from the sago palm and can be made into a kind of bread; yams; fruits like mango, banana, and coconut; and fish.

Fiji

Moving on through the Pacific Ocean, we come to Fiji, a group of 322 islands and 522 islets, or small islands. The main islands of Viti Levu and Vanua Levu contain most of the country's population. Fiji is also a part of Melanesia.

ALL ABOUT
Papua New Guinea

Capital and largest city: Port Moresby

Official languages: English, Tok Pisin, and Hiri Motu

Area: 178,703 square miles

Population: 6.7 million (2007 estimate)

BIRDS OF PARADISE: Birds of paradise are very colorful birds with long feathers, or plumes, in their tails. The males display their beautiful plumes to attract the plain female birds.

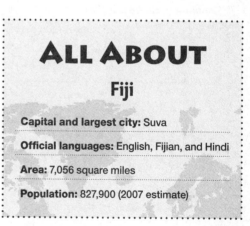

ALL ABOUT
Fiji

Capital and largest city: Suva

Official languages: English, Fijian, and Hindi

Area: 7,056 square miles

Population: 827,900 (2007 estimate)

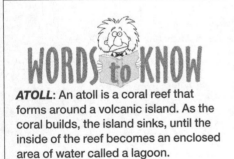

Kwajalein Atoll

Kwajalein is one of the world's largest coral atolls, with a land area of six square miles. It has one of the largest lagoons, too.

ALL ABOUT

The Marshall Islands

Capital and largest city: Majuro

Official languages: Marshallese and English

Area: 70 square miles

Population: 52,338 (2006 estimate)

WORDS to KNOW

ATOLL: An atoll is a coral reef that forms around a volcanic island. As the coral builds, the island sinks, until the inside of the reef becomes an enclosed area of water called a lagoon.

The climate in Fiji is tropical and warm all year long. The dense rainforests on the southeastern sides of the islands are battered by heavy rains, up to 120 inches per year. Much of the terrain is mountainous, and the larger islands have peaks as high as 4,000 feet. These peaks protect the lowlands and enable a dry season in which to grow crops such as sugar, which is a big industry for Fiji.

Mining and tourism are also big industries, but many of the people still rely on farming. While the population of Fiji consists mostly of native Fijians, there are also Indo-Fijians who are of Indian origin. As a result, the culture in this country is quite varied, including traditions from India, China, and Europe.

The Marshall Islands

At last we come to the Marshall Islands, which are part of Micronesia. Made up of 29 atolls and five separate islands, the Marshall Islands have a tropical climate with a wet season from May to November. The islands are often hit by tropical storms called typhoons, because most of the terrain is at sea level.

The economy in the Marshall Islands is mainly agricultural, in which small farms grow commercial crops such as coconuts, tomatoes, and melons, among other foods. At one point, fishing was an important industry, and the Marshallese were skilled canoe builders. There are annual races with a special kind of ocean canoe called a *proa*.

Brrrrrrr!

The world's lowest recorded temperature was –129 degrees, at Vostok Research Station in Antarctica in 1983. Inland temperatures can go down to –112 to –130 degrees in winter, and coastal temperatures can go up to between 41 and 59 degrees in summer.

ALL ABOUT

All about Antarctica

Overall area: 5.41 million square miles

Area without ice: 108,109 square miles

Area with ice: 5.3 million square miles

Highest point: Vinson Massif, 16,067 feet

Lowest point: sea level

Antarctica

In our travels, we've visited some amazing countries, met all kinds of people, and learned about unusual and fascinating animals. Our last stop is a continent with almost no people at all and only a few animals. Antarctica is the largest desert in the world—a cold, desolate expanse of ice and snow. In this chapter, we'll learn about the climate and the scientific research in Antarctica, we'll travel to the North and South Poles to meet some penguins and other cold-weather animals, and we'll learn how global warming is affecting this icy world. So bundle up nice and warm. Let's go to Antarctica!

The Bottom of the World

The fifth-biggest continent in the world, Antarctica is the coldest, driest, and windiest place on Earth. It is almost completely covered in the Antarctic ice sheet, which ranges from one to three miles thick. There's a lot of frozen water in all that snow. But Antarctica is called a desert because it only gets a little precipitation—about the same amount as the Sahara in Africa! One reason it's so cold in Antarctica, besides all the snow and ice, is that freezing winds called katabatic winds blow up to 200 miles per hour. These winds blow from high plateaus down onto the coasts and cause strong blizzards.

Antarctica has the world's largest ice shelves: the Ross Ice Shelf and the Filchner-Ronne Ice Shelf. An ice shelf is a thick section of ice that forms at the spot where a glacier or ice sheet meets the coastline. The Ross Ice Shelf is 2,300 feet thick in some places, and the Filchner-Ronne Ice Shelf is about 2,000 feet at its thickest. In summer, ice shelves melt and break way, forming icebergs. Some Antarctic icebergs are as big as 5,000 square miles.

Turn Out the Lights

If you look at a map of Earth, you can see five major latitude lines. One of them is the Antarctic Circle. In the Northern Hemisphere, there is a similar line called the Arctic Circle. South of the Antarctic Circle, in Antarctica, there is one day of constant sunlight and one day of no sunlight every year. This happens because of how the earth is tilted in relation to the sun. These days are called solstices, and one happens in winter and one happens in summer. Winter in the Southern Hemisphere lasts from May through September. Summer lasts from November through February.

No Snow?

Travel inland from the coasts, and you'll find the highest average elevation of all the other continents and the least precipitation. Several mountains make up the long line of Transantarctic Mountains that separate East Antarctica and West Antarctica. One of the longer ranges on Earth, it is 2,175 miles long, stretching from the Ross Sea to the Weddell Sea. Surprisingly, though, the summits and dry valleys of the Transantarctic Mountains are not covered by ice because winds blow away any snow that falls and the area receives so little precipitation. The highest peak here is Mount Kirkpatrick, at 14,856 feet, located in the Queen Alexandra Range. The highest mountain range is the Ellsworth Mountains, which form a chain that is 200 miles long and 30 miles wide, and whose highest peak is Vinson Massif, at 16,050 feet. Vinson Massif is the highest point on the continent of Antarctica.

Antarctica is also home to several volcanoes, most of them dormant. But one, Mount Erebus, is the southernmost active volcano in the world. It stands 12,448 feet tall and it is located on Ross Island. It is part of the Pacific Ring of Fire.

DID YOU KNOW?

Sunburn from Snow

You can get sunburned even in winter, because the snow reflects the sunlight onto your skin. Make sure you wear sunscreen when you're playing in the snow on a sunny day!

TRY THIS

Sunny Bedtime

The next time you're getting ready to go to bed, imagine what it would be like to have bright sunshine outside. How would you sleep? Then, in the morning, imagine you're waking up to complete darkness outside. What would you do all day if there was no sunlight at all?

WORDS to KNOW

SOLSTICE: The word solstice comes from two Latin words: *sol* (sun) and *sistere* (to stand still), meaning the sun looks as though it's not moving. A solstice is either a day of all sunlight or a day of all darkness.

Tropical Antarctica?

More than 500 million years ago, Antarctica was part of a larger land mass called Gondwana, and West Antarctica was north of the equator. The continent had a warm, tropical climate with all kinds of animals, including some dinosaurs!

Research Stations

If you look around you, you won't see houses, driveways, cars, or bicycles. Nobody lives here all year long. The only people here are scientists, who live in special buildings called research stations. Some research stations are underground to help keep them warm. The scientists keep enough food, water, and medical supplies to last them a year, even if that's longer than they think they'll stay, because the weather is unpredictable. At any moment, a blizzard may strike and prevent planes or helicopters from dropping off any more supplies. In addition, the temperatures are so cold that pilots can only stay on the ground for a little while before their fuel begins to freeze. If that happens, they cannot take off and they're stuck, too.

What do these researchers do here? Well, despite the cold and the winds and the lack of rain, there are some animals that have learned to survive here. Some researchers come to study how these animals have adapted to such a harsh environment. Other scientists study the ice itself to find tiny organisms that are trapped inside. In Antarctica, there are about 70 lakes under the ice sheet, some of which have been buried for hundreds of thousands of years. Perhaps if there are organisms still alive in these lakes, there might be similar organisms living on parts of our solar system that are just as frozen and barren, such as Europa, a cold moon of Jupiter.

Welcome to the South Pole!

The South Pole is located near the center of the continent of Antarctica, on a cold area of flat land that is covered in snow. At an altitude of 9,301 feet, the ice at the pole is estimated to be about 9,000 feet thick. The polar ice sheet moves very slowly each year toward the Weddell Sea, so the exact position of the South

The EVERYTHING KIDS' Geography Book

Pole changes over time. The geographical South Pole is marked by a small sign and a stake that are moved every year on New Year's Day to the pole's new location. Written on the sign are the dates Roald Amundsen and Robert F. Scott arrived at the South Pole, quotes from both men, and the elevation. There is also a Ceremonial South Pole marker, intended for photos, that is moved relative to the geographical South Pole so that they remain near one another.

Roald Amundsen, from Norway, and Robert F. Scott, from Great Britain, were the first explorers to reach the South Pole, Amundsen arriving a month ahead of Scott. U.S. Admiral Richard Evelyn Bird flew over the South Pole in 1929. There have been many expeditions to the South Pole since then, by land and by air.

In the summer, though the sun is always present, it sits just above the horizon and it gives off very little warmth. That's why the South Pole has one of the coldest climates on Earth. It is much colder than the North Pole, because the altitude at the South Pole is higher than at the North Pole. At the Amundsen-Scott South Pole Station, the highest temperature ever recorded was 7.5 degrees and the lowest was –117 degrees.

The climate of the South Pole is similar to the rest of inland Antarctica. There is very little precipitation, and wind gusts blow the snow around into piles called drifts. They can add up to around eight inches. There are no animals or plants at the South Pole itself, since the weather is too harsh. However, later in this chapter we'll look at some animals that do live along the coasts of Antarctica.

The North Pole: I'm on Top of the World!

The North Pole is located in the center of the Arctic Ocean, in the middle of floating ice. There are no permanent research stations at the North Pole, but there are some drifting stations, which are structures built on

Pick a Pole

Our world has two north poles. One is geographic and one is magnetic. This explorer is using her compass to find the magnetic north pole. Can you see how to get there?

North Pole

- Go three steps east.
- Go three steps north.
- Go two steps east.
- Go four steps north.
- Go one step west.
- Go two steps north.
- Go three steps west, and there you are!

Start

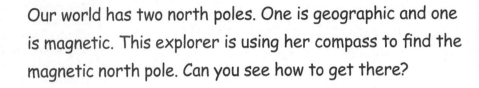

In the Dark For 186 days of the year, the sun does not appear at the North Pole.

The Arctic isn't really the top of the world. Viewed from outer space, just like a ball, there is no top or bottom, north or south.

The EVERYTHING KIDS' Geography Book

large sheets of ice in the ocean. Scientists in these floating buildings measure the ocean, learn about marine life, and more. Can you imagine doing experiments on a floating piece of ice? Near the North Pole, the sea is about 13,980 feet deep. The nearest shore is Greenland, about 440 miles away.

Robert E. Peary is believed to be the first explorer to reach the North Pole, on April 6, 1909. He and his team—an American named Matthew Henson and four Inuit men—traveled by dogsled. Many trips to the pole, both on foot and in the air, have been questioned. Sometimes it's hard to be sure whether the person arrived at just the right spot. But the first proven sighting of the North Pole was on May 12, 1926, by Amundsen and another man named Lincoln Ellsworth from an airship called the *Norge*. This made Amundsen the first person to reach both the North and South Poles.

The Arctic region is harsh and cold, though not as cold as Antarctica. However, not many people live here. Among those that do live in this region are the Sami of northern Scandinavia, the Yugyts and Nenets of Siberia, and the Inuit of Canada. Some of these people still lead nomadic lives. They hunt animals for food and use them for all their basic needs, such as tools and clothing. Others live in cities, leading more settled lives.

Penguins, Seals, Whales, and More!

There are all kinds of amazing animals that survive the cold in Antarctica and in the Arctic. We're going to learn about penguins, blue whales, seals, polar bears—the only land animal in the Arctic—and the amazing Arctic tern.

Dressed for the Weather

There are 17 species of penguins around the world, but in Antarctica the best known is the Emperor penguin. They are the biggest penguins in the world, standing about 48 inches tall and weighing anywhere from 48 to 82 pounds.

Posing Penguins

In the vast open spaces of Antarctica, penguins have to be able to distinguish their partner or baby. These two are about to go explore a glacier. Can you find the 8 differences between the leader and the follower?*

*Facing a different direction doesn't count as a difference.

They have black feathers on their backs, white feathers on their bellies, and yellow feathers around their necks. Like all penguins, they are excellent swimmers and can dive up to 1,755 feet for food, remaining underwater for up to 18 minutes. They eat fish and squid.

When Emperor penguins are ready to mate and take care of their young, a female Emperor hands off her egg to her mate by gently nudging it from her flippers to his. It is important that the egg never touch the frozen ice. Then the female waddles back to the sea in search of food. The male remains with a large colony of as many as 6,000 other father penguins, all prepared to face the bitter Antarctic winter and care for their eggs. The male tucks the egg under a flap of warm skin to protect it from the cold. He will stay in that position for the next 64 days until the egg hatches. Biting winds howl around the huddled penguins, who rotate in and out of the center of the group for warmth. Male penguins may lose up to 44 pounds during this time. They cannot leave to get food or water. At long last, the female penguins, having eaten quite a bit during this time, make the journey back to the penguin colony to take care of their chicks. When the chicks hatch, if the female has not yet returned, the male can cough up a tiny bit of food to keep the chick alive. A female can find her mate by his calls. Finally, the male can leave to find food, making the same journey to the sea.

Other penguin species in Antarctica include Chinstrap penguins, Adelie penguins, Gentoo penguins, King penguins, and Macaroni penguins.

The EVERYTHING KIDS' Geography Book

Whale of a Tail

What's the largest animal that ever lived? The blue whale, of course! Growing up to 100 feet long, blue whales are baleen whales that feed on krill, which are tiny shrimp-like creatures that swim in the ocean. Whales are mammals, not fish, even though they live their entire lives in the water. They have lungs, they breathe air through their blowholes, and they give milk to their babies. During the summer in Antarctica, blue whales feed in the southern oceans, and then they migrate north during the Arctic summer to breed.

Seals

There are six species of seals found in the Antarctic area, but only four are considered native: the Weddell, the Ross, the Crabeater, and the Leopard. The Southern Elephant seal and the Fur seal sometimes come to Antarctica but spend most of their time elsewhere. Let's look at the Leopard seal.

The Leopard seal is the largest of the native Antarctic seals. They are also the most aggressive and will hunt and kill other seals. They can grow to be 10 feet long and weigh up to 750 pounds. They have black spots on their grey bodies, giving them their name. Their long, sharp teeth, their strong and narrow bodies, and their excellent senses of sight and smell underwater make them excellent predators. Their main food is penguins, but they will also eat fish, squid, and krill.

The Great White Bear

Following the tern up north, we come to the land of the polar bears. These bears are the largest land predators. Males can grow to the enormous size of 1,500 pounds and reach lengths of almost 10 feet. A polar bear's ears and tail are small, but his paws are big and wide to help him stay above the ice as he walks. These paws also help the polar bear swim. He has thick fur

BALEEN: Baleen is a comb-like structure in a whale's mouth that it uses instead of teeth to pick krill and fish from the gulps of water it drinks.

Fun Fact

The Tiniest Largest Land Animal

Because of the severe conditions of inland Antarctica, the only animal that lives year-round on land is the wingless midge, a tiny insect less than a half-inch long. No need for wings when there are gusty winds all around!

When Ice Attacks!

The largest floating object on Earth ran aground in Antarctica in 2005. This bottle-shaped iceberg was 120 kilometers in length—about half the distance from London to Paris. See who was in danger because of where the iceberg landed—just cross out the boxes with the words that fit these descriptions.

Types of shirts

Words with a double "l"

Words with the same letter at the start and the end

Types of boats

Words that are the opposite of fat

Things you use when you swim

TEE	NOON	SAIL	PENGUINS	SKINNY
SWALLOW	COULDN'T	THIN	GET	PILLOW
PLUMP	CANOE	TO	FLUFF	THE
GOGGLES	SEA	GOLF	FLIPPER	TO
KAYAK	FIND	LLAMA	SWEAT	FOOD

The EVERYTHING KIDS' Geography Book

and blubber, a kind of fat, to keep him warm and afloat in the cold waters of the Arctic. He also has an excellent sense of smell, which he uses to find seals under the ice. A polar bear stands near a hole in the ice that seals use to pop out of the water and take a breath. The bear waits until he can smell a seal exhale before leaving the water. Then the bear snatches the seal out of the hole for dinner. Bears will sometimes roam thousands of miles to find seals, though they usually stay within a much smaller range. Many other arctic animals depend upon polar bears for their dinner, including Arctic foxes and gulls that eat leftovers from a bear's meal.

What Is Happening to Our Ice?

Now let's explore what's happening to the icy worlds of the Arctic and the Antarctic because of global warming.

Global Warming

Remember the scientists on the research stations on Antarctica? Some of them are interested in what the ice can tell them about the history of Antarctica. What was the Earth's atmosphere like hundreds or thousands or millions of years ago? Answering this question can help them understand how the atmosphere has changed in recent years. These scientists have done studies that tell them we have too many greenhouse gases in the atmosphere—especially carbon dioxide. Many scientists believe this comes from pollution from our factories and our cars. Too much carbon dioxide traps heat near the surface of the planet instead of letting that heat escape, and this warms the temperature of the planet. If the planet warms up too much, all the ice may melt, causing water levels to rise in the oceans and seas, flooding cities and affecting plants, animals, and humans.

In Antarctica, some of the ice is already melting, despite the cold temperatures. When the ice melts, it breaks off of the main continent and

floats out into the ocean. This is dangerous because the ice gets in the way of ships, and melted ice raises the level of the oceans. The Antarctic continent has 90 percent of the world's ice and 70 percent of the world's fresh water. If all this ice were to melt, the levels of the seas would rise by about 200 feet. This would be more than enough to flood coastal cities like New York City and make them unlivable.

Home Sweet Home

Another problem with melting ice is loss of habitat. For the polar bear in the Arctic, the ice provides a platform for hunting seals. When the temperatures go up too early in the year, they lose their platform and are forced to swim for miles to find another area of ice. Or the bears have to come ashore for the summer before they've eaten enough food to keep them full through the difficult warm months. If the bears are malnourished, then they won't reproduce as much, and the bear population goes down. In addition, mother bears depend on the ice to make dens for their cubs. When the ice melts earlier in the year, the mothers have to swim further distances to find good ice to make their dens. As food becomes scarce, the bears make their way into towns to scavenge in garbage cans. This results in encounters between humans and bears, which is dangerous.

Experts say we need to cut down on the amount of fossil fuels we use, such as oil and gasoline, if we want to slow the effects of global warming and help our polar regions. Here's a challenge. Think of three ways you can personally use less fossil fuels. Maybe you can walk or ride your bike to school instead of having your parents drive you. Maybe you can recycle your newspaper, cans, and bottles so they can be reused; this takes fewer fossil fuels than making materials from scratch. Take charge and look around your community for ways to help our planet and save the ice!

Resources

Want to learn even more about the countries you have read about in this book? Check out these websites!

CIA—World Factbook

The Central Intelligence Agency has a World Factbook online. This fact book includes data and information about every country in the world, including facts about the people, geography, and economics of each country. Go to the CIA's main website and click on the link for the World Factbook. *www.cia.gov*

National Geographic

Check out the National Geographic Society website and learn about the world! You may be familiar with the well-known magazine, *National Geographic*. This website is produced and maintained by the same organization. At this site you will find information about different cultures, history, animals, and people from around the world. Go to the site and spend some time clicking around. You'll be amazed at what you find! *www.nationalgeographic.com*

World Atlas

Looking for a resource for quick information about any country in the world? Are you curious about what the flag of a country may look like or what currency they use? Then look no further than this website. Worldatltas.com includes information about all these topics and many others. *www.worldatlas.com*

Test Your Geography Knowledge

Feeling confident about your geography knowledge? Try one of the quizzes on this website. There are quizzes to test your knowledge of the continents, countries, and capital cities. You may want to have a copy of Appendix B available while you take these quizzes! *www.lizardpoint.com/fun/geoquiz*

APPENDIX B
Puzzle Solutions

Simple Symbol • page 5

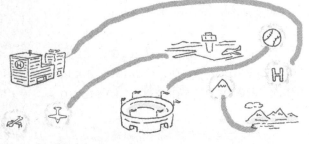

Mousey Messy Maze • page 7

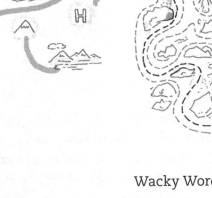

Island I.D • page 9

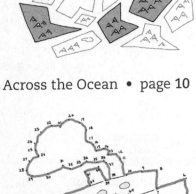

Wacky Words • page 17

Mountain moving makes men miss Missouri.
Cowardly Colorado cows chew cuds.
Angels are attracting ants in Arizona.
Why would wise women wander Wymoning?
Illinois isn't in Indiana, is it?

Across the Ocean • page 10

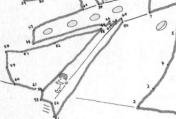

Mini Mountain • page 19

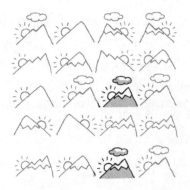

The EVERYTHING KIDS' Geography Book

Fractured Faults • page 24

```
A U L T F A U L T F L A T
F A F A U L F A L T U F U
T L U F U A L T F A U T L
A F L F A U L T U A L T Y
U F U A T F U A L T F F A
F T L U A F T L U F L U T
A A F L U A L F U A L T A
U F U T U A F L A F L F T
L T U A F T L U A T F A U
F A U F A L U T U L U A F
F A U T L U A F A U T L F
```

Mexican Marvel • page 32

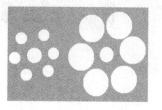

The circles are
the same size.

Shape Shifter • page 34

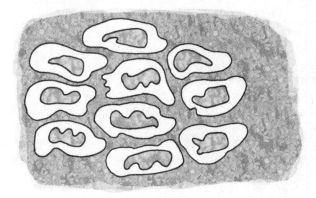

Discover Cove • page 29

The Fastest Game on Earth • page 38

American Records • page 46

Driest desert

Island Hopping • page 48

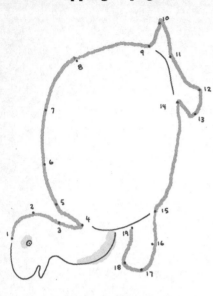

Hills and Valleys • page 56

Bay - Baia (Portuguese)
Mountain - Berg (German)
Valley - Valle (Italian)
Border - Granica (Polish)
Volcano - Vulkaan (Dutch)
Desert - Desierto (Spanish)
Beach - Plage (French)

Alps • page 62

Pure Europe • page 53

ape, are, ear, era, ere, Euro, Europe, nap, nape, neap, near, nope, nor, ore, one, open, opera, our, pan, pane, par, pare, pea, pear, peer, pen, peon, per, Peru, pone, pore, pour, preen, prone, prune, pure, ran, reap, roe, roan, rope, run, rupee

The country that is shaped like a boot is Italy.

Cave Code • page 65

Only Opposite • page 61

Under - Over
Deep - Shallow
Solid - Molten
Full - Empty
Dry - Wet
Valley - Mountain
Smooth - Rough

Dry Skies • page 72

Form Features • page 70

Canals and ports are not landforms because they are manmade.

The EVERYTHING KIDS' Geography Book

Make It "To Go" • page 74

Living Dangerously • page 79

Name That Country! • page 88

The Great White North - Canada

Down Under - Australia

Emerald Isle - Ireland

Land of the Long White
Cloud - New Zealand

Land of the Free, Home of
the Brave - USA

Land of the Thunder
Dragon – China

The Sleeping Giant -
South Korea

Land of the Midnight
Sun - Iceland

Longest Largest • page 84

Yangtze (China): 3,917 miles
Yellow (China): 3,398 miles
Lena (Russia): 2,736 miles
Volga (Russia): 2,266 miles
Indus (Pakistan and India): 1,976 miles

The Yangtze is often called the
dirtiest river in Asia.

Lucky House • page 90

12 dragons

African E-mail • page 94

Copy Continent • page 98

Spelling Sailors • page 100

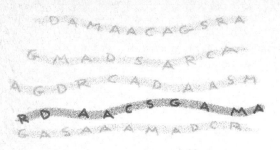

Add Up Australia • page 109

There are eleven deserts in Australia.

Ayers Rock is 5.5 miles around at its base.

Strangeray Springs is 30,029 square kilometers.

The Great Barrier Reef is made up of 2,900 reefs.

Bubble Trouble • page 116

Posing Penguins • page 126

Devil in Disguise • page 112

Pick a Pole • page 124

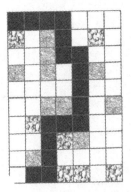

When Ice Attacks! • page 128

TEE	NOON	SAIL	PENGUINS	SKINNY
SWALLOW	COULDN'T	THIN	GET	PILLOW
PLUMP	CANOE	TO	FLUFF	THE
GOGGLES	SEA	GOLF	FLIPPER	TO
KAYAK	FIND	LLAMA	SWEAT	FOOD

The EVERYTHING KIDS' Geography Book